Pablo Neruda
Block print by Carlos Hermosilla Alvárez

The Poetry of
Pablo
Neruda

The Poetry of

Pablo Neruda

René de Costa

HARVARD UNIVERSITY PRESS
Cambridge, Massachusetts
and London, England
1979

Publication of this book has been aided by a
grant from the Andrew W. Mellon Foundation

**Library of Congress Cataloging in
Publication Data**

Costa, René de.
The poetry of Pablo Neruda.

Bibliography: p.
Includes index.
1.   Neruda, Pablo, 1904–1973—Criticism and
interpretation.   I.   Title.
PQ8097.N4Z615   861   78–18008
ISBN 0–674–67980–6

Selections from the Spanish CREPUSCULARIO by Pablo Neruda, Santiago de
Chile, 1923. From VEINTE POEMAS DE AMOR by Pablo Neruda, Santiago de
Chile, 1924. From TENTATIVA DEL HOMBRE INFINITO by Pablo Neruda,
Santiago de Chile, 1926. From CANTO GENERAL by Pablo Neruda, © Editorial
Losada, S.A., Buenos Aires, 1955. From ODAS ELEMENTALES by Pablo Neruda,
© Editorial Losada, 1958. From ESTRAVAGARIO by Pablo Neruda, © Editorial
Losada, 1958. Translated by René de Costa. English language translation Copyright
© 1978 by Farrar, Straus & Giroux, Inc. Reprinted with the permission of Farrar,
Straus & Giroux, Inc., and Souvenir Press, Ltd., London.
    Selections from Pablo Neruda, RESIDENCE ON EARTH. Copyright © 1958,
1961, 1962 by Editorial Losada, S.A., Buenos Aires. Reprinted by permission of
Agencia Literaria Carmen Balcells (Barcelona) and New Directions.
    Permission granted by Grove Press for the use of "Por fin se fueron"; "Los Poetas
celestes"; and "La United Fruit Co."
    Lines from "Amor América," "Oda a una castaña en el suelo," and "El Miedo,"
excerpted from the book PABLO NERUDA: *Selected Poems,* edited by Nathaniel
Tarn. Copyright © 1972 by Dell Publishing Co., Inc. Reprinted by permission of
Delacorte Press / Seymour Lawrence.

for Serpil

Preface

Just a few months before Neruda's untimely death in September 1973, Losada, South America's largest publishing house, had thoroughly updated its standard edition of the poet's complete works. In three weighty tomes, on thin bible paper, this, the fourth edition of the *Obras completas de Pablo Neruda,* comprising more than 3,500 pages and some thirty-four books of poetry, drama, and essays, will not be the last, for at this writing an additional nine volumes of verse and a book of memoirs have appeared posthumously. A veritable river of print, which presents, and represents, an entire life in literature—fifty years, to be exact, since it was in 1923 that the young Neruda, a nineteen-year-old dropout in French literature at the University of Chile, published his first book, *Crepusculario.* Since then his output has been truly phenomenal—not merely because of its almost torrential quantity, but mostly because of its regularly outstanding quality.

Today, in retrospect, certain volumes stand out above the rest and seem to mark off more than a few high points in the overall evolution of twentieth-century poetry in Spanish: *Veinte poemas de amor y una canción desesperada, Residencia en la tierra, Canto general,* and *Odas elementales,* to name only the most prominent, those most clearly identifiable as modern-day classics. Each of these volumes once signaled something radically new and different in the development of Hispanic poetry, and inevitably, inexorably, represented for the poet a break with his past, with the very literary tradition he had come to personify. Such a process has not been without difficulties, probably for the poet and certainly for his critics and translators. The attainment of a particular style and its subsequent appreciation and acceptance by his readers and emulators seems only to have served Neruda as a renewed impetus for change, a command to go beyond his own achievement, to surpass himself once again. He even referred to himself once as the "foremost adversary of Nerudism."*

This dynamic need to change, central to Neruda's development as a writer, has resulted in a work so vast and varied that it seems to thwart any attempt to synthesize it, to discipline it into a single unifying scheme. One problem for the critic has been that Neruda's writing does not evolve in the traditional way, according to a smooth trajectory of growth and refinement. Instead, after each triumph there is a series of spurts, of experimental compositions, followed by a volcanic outflow of verses that result in a totally new book and, to be sure, a new and somewhat different poetic. Another, related, problem is that while Neruda's first poems were intensely lyrical and personal, much of his later work was fiercely political and public. What is more, midway through his career as a poet-diplomat he joined the Communist Party and became a poet-politician, being elected to the Chilean Senate in 1946 and, more recently, serving his party as the pre-candidate for the Presidency in the 1970 elections that brought Salvador Allende to power.

Neruda's extraordinary propensity for change and his deepening political involvement have over the years had a peculiar effect on the criticism of his work, which is now quite extensive: more than thirty books and thousands upon thousands of arti-

---

* Unpublished speech delivered at the University of Chile in January 1954; quoted in Margarita Aguirre, *Las vidas de Pablo Neruda* (Santiago, Zig-Zag, 1967), p. 277.

cles, studies, and reviews. Neruda's writing has stimulated many
to write about it and him, and for diverse and often partisan
reasons. Thus, there are many critics who, esteeming the lyrical
and metaphysical qualities of the earlier work, find fault with
the later poetry of social commitment; others, sympathetic with
the author's political concerns, exalt only the more militant
aspects of his writing; and yet others prefer to eschew politics
almost entirely in their criticism, by studying the treatment
accorded certain grand themes, like love and death. Such a
divergence of critical viewpoints is perhaps to be expected,
given the richness and variety of Neruda's work over the past
half-century. But what is needed now, I believe, is an integrative
view, a nonpartisan reassessment of each work considered to be
major, the political and the nonpolitical, so as to determine its
uniqueness in the larger context of modern poetry as well as its
proper place in the more personal context of Neruda's total
oeuvre. This is what I have attempted to do in this book.

For this reason, I have not argued a thesis, nor have I tried to
explain all the works of Pablo Neruda, which would be a
monumental task. My intention is more modest: to lay the
groundwork for agreement on the literary significance of the
major works by examining them in detail in an effort to point
out just why they are, or were, major. To do this most effectively,
to assess with some degree of accuracy the contextual significance
of the books which are truly epochal, I have found it useful to
return to the original editions—Neruda was an inveterate re-
viser—and to cull the periodical literature of the past in order
to situate each item in its proper context, the socioaesthetic
context of its own time. In this way the specific quality of each
of the major poetic styles once championed by the author be-
comes most apparent, and each of Neruda's many voices can be
seen to be synthesized in a single literary masterwork and a
singular authorial posture: the neoromantic of *Veinte poemas
de amor y una canción desesperada* (1924), the vanguardist of
Tentativa del hombre infinito (1926), the anguished existential-
ist of *Residencia en la tierra* (1933), the socially committed in-
tellectual of *Tercera residencia* (1947), the epic voice of America

in *Canto general* (1950), the plain lyricist of the *Odas elementales* (1954), and, finally, the colloquial anti-poet of *Estravagario* (1958) and beyond. Each of these works posed a unique set of literary problems for the reader of its time. However, each work also contained an equally unique and aesthetically valid set of responses to the very questions it posed. Therefore, in the chapters that follow I shall be focusing attention on these, the identifiably major works, in an effort to guide the reader of today toward a greater comprehension and appreciation of the dynamics of change and continuity in the poetry of Pablo Neruda.

Neruda's poetry has transcended Chile, and, indeed, the Hispanic world. For this reason I have provided, for the benefit of the reader who may not know Spanish, my own plain-prose literal translation of all the poems quoted. (Excellent verse translations of many of them may be found in the volumes listed on page 208 and in *Pablo Neruda, Selected Poems: A Bilingual Edition,* Delacorte Press/Seymour Lawrence, 1972.) Prose quotations are given in English only, again in my own translation. Footnotes have been kept to a minimum; the bibliography refers to the books and articles I have found most useful and recommend for further reading.

I would like to recognize my debt to all those who have written on Neruda before me. Their many ideas and opinions, although impossible to acknowledge individually, have in one way or another contributed toward the shaping of my own. I would also like to express a special debt of gratitude to my colleagues and friends, Sheldon Sacks, Ricardo Gullón, Paolo Cherchi, Pedro Lastra, José Emilio Pacheco, and Humberto Robles, who read the manuscript at various stages of its elaboration and offered much helpful advice toward its improvement. Thanks must also go to my students at the University of Chicago whose probing questions helped transform my lecture notes into this book.

APRIL 1978   R. DE C.
CHICAGO

Contents

Illustrations

Grateful acknowledgment is made to Carlos Hermosilla Alvárez, for permission to reproduce his engraving of Neruda in the frontispiece, and to Margarita Aguirre, who has generously drawn on her Neruda archives for the other iconographic material illustrating this book.

The Poetry of
Pablo
Neruda

1. Introduction
The Major Works

> One by one, I have been leaving my books behind
> me, substituting, reconstructing form and meaning
> each time. I am the foremost adversary of Nerudism.
>
> *1954*

Neruda was a poet of many styles and many voices, one whose multitudinous work is central to almost every important development in twentieth-century Spanish and Spanish American poetry. He was once referred to as the Picasso of poetry, alluding to his protean ability to be always in the vanguard of change. And he himself has often alluded to his personal struggle with his own tradition, to his constant need to search for a new system of expression in each new book. Neruda was, until very recently in his later years, a poet perpetually in revolution against himself, against his own tradition. Perhaps for this reason he frequently had difficulties in finding an initial acceptance for so many of the works today recognized as major.

In fact, the most famous of all his books, a text that has thus far sold several million copies and has gone through countless editions since it first appeared in Santiago over fifty years ago, was once considered unpublishable. I am referring to *Veinte poemas de amor y una canción desesperada* (Twenty Love Poems and a Song of Despair). In 1923, just after the polite, but positive, critical reception of the traditional verses of his first book, *Crepusculario,* the Chilean publishing house Nascimento refused to print the love poems. At the time it was felt that they were too "erotic" and that their publication would tarnish the good reputation of the press. Neruda's straightforward celebra-

1

tion of love, lovemaking, and the longing to make love was considered to be a bit too direct, hence, not sufficiently "poetic." Significantly enough, the controversial quality of the work then can help us to appreciate its uniqueness now.

Love and sex, to be sure, have long been traditional subjects of poetry. However, the treatment of the erotic theme is usually quite conventional. Euphemism and metaphor are used to abstract and idealize the erogenous parts of the body, while passion is somehow artistically sublimated in a kind of mystic enthrallment before the beloved. Neruda's book of 1924 challenged this genteel tradition. Idealism was replaced by sensualism, abstraction by concreteness. In *Veinte poemas de amor* love was not sentimental and unrequited as in the Petrarchian model; rather erotic passion and the sensual delights of the flesh were openly exalted. Thus, "Cuerpo de Mujer" (Body of Woman), the first of the twenty love poems is not written to a courtly idol; not to the conventional parts of the female anatomy made familiar by poetic tradition; not to eyes like diamonds, teeth like pearls, skin like alabaster or marble—images that the reader of love poetry since the Renaissance has almost wearily come to expect. It is to the body of woman, any woman, all women. Neruda unceremoniously set aside all these poetic conventions to celebrate the call of anonymous flesh and carnal pleasure. "Cuerpo de mujer" sets the tone of the entire book:

> Cuerpo de mujer, blancas colinas, muslos blancos,
> te pareces al mundo en tu actitud de entrega.
> Mi cuerpo de labriego salvaje te socava
> y hace saltar el hijo del fondo de la tierra.

> Fui solo como un túnel. De mí huían los pájaros,
> y en mí la noche entraba su invasión poderosa.
> Para sobrevivirme te forjé como un arma,
> como una flecha en mi arco, como una piedra en mi honda.

> Pero cae la hora de la venganza, y te amo.
> Cuerpo de piel, de musgo, de leche ávida y firme.
> Ah los vasos del pecho! Ah los ojos de ausencia!
> Ah las rosas del pubis! Ah tu voz lenta y triste!

Cuerpo de mujer mía, persistiré en tu gracia.
Mi sed, mi ansia sin límite, mi camino indeciso!
Oscuros cauces donde la sed eterna sigue,
y la fatiga sigue, y el dolor infinito.

Body of woman, white hills, white thighs, you resemble the world in your attitude of giving. My rough peasant body digs in you and makes the son leap from the depth of the earth.   I went alone like a tunnel. The birds fled from me, and night swamped me with its crushing invasion. To survive I forged you like a weapon, like an arrow in my bow, a stone in my sling.   But the hour of vengeance falls, and I love you. Body of skin, of moss, of eager and firm milk. Ah, the goblets of your breast! Ah, the eyes of absence! Ah, the roses of your pubis! Ah, your voice so slow and sad!   Body of my woman, I will persist in your grace. My thirst, my limitless desire, my undecided path! Dark riverbeds where the eternal thirst flows, and weariness flows, and the infinite ache.

Neruda was convinced that this poetry of passionate longing was artistically significant, and when the manuscript was rejected by the publisher he appealed to the established literary figures for support. In Chile it was the chaste and aristocratic Pedro Prado who responded. It is hard to imagine the author of the delicate *Alsino* supporting such erotic audacity, yet in the archives of the Prado family in Santiago there is an interesting letter from Neruda to Prado concerning the difficulties with the publisher. Pedro Prado was then Director of Chile's Museum of Fine Arts and one of the country's more prestigious writers. In this 1923 letter Neruda complains bitterly about Nascimento's refusal to print the love poems and his unsuccessful efforts with other Chilean publishing houses. Neruda was even willing to pay to have the book printed—but it seems that no one would have it under any conditions. The letter concludes with a prophetic phrase, which at the time must have seemed audacious, motivated as it was by resentment and youthful bravado. Neruda writes: "Le pesará, les pesará a todos" (He'll be sorry;

they'll all be sorry). The owner of the publishing house didn't have to be sorry, however, because Prado convinced him that he should risk publishing the young Neruda's book of love poems. And so, it finally did come out the following year, in 1924, to the shock and delight of the critics and reading public. The book has since sold millions and millions of copies, establishing in the process a new readership and a new diction for love poetry in Spanish.

In 1926, with the enthusiastic support of Nascimento and the Chilean avant-garde, Neruda published another book of poetry, *Tentativa del hombre infinito* (Venture of the Infinite Man), a major work that until quite recently has been somewhat misunderstood. Critics who liked his love poetry were at first dismayed by this book, for in it Neruda seemed to have abandoned not only rhyme and meter but also, according to some, any semblance of meaning. The problem was that in an effort to purify his poetic language, to rid it entirely of the hollow rhetoric of the past, he created a work that was so strange and unfamiliar to most readers of the time that they were unable and unwilling to make any sense out of it. The volume's opening lines are certainly as unusual as any:

> hogueras pálidas revolviéndose al borde de las noches
> corren humos difuntos polvaredas invisibles

> pallid fires turning about at the edge of the nights dead smoke
> invisible dust clouds race on.

Today Surrealism has left us with an appreciation for the suggestive power of discontinuous discourse, and these lines, evoking the disquiet of a nocturnal scene, are not nearly so cryptic as was once believed. In retrospect it is possible to see that the techniques Neruda employed in this early experimental work actually foreshadow those of *Residencia en la tierra* (Residence on Earth), which was not published until much later, in 1933.

In 1927 Neruda abandoned Santiago and the Chilean avant-garde to take up his first diplomatic appointment, consul to far-off Rangoon, Burma—not exactly a prized post at the time. The years he lived in the Far East were extremely difficult. Without a salary, living on a few meager consular fees, and without any Spanish-speaking friends he was virtually isolated in an alien culture. He was forced to turn inward, and, as a consequence, he wrote somewhat less urgently and with an even more concentrated intensity, practicing a kind of intimate dialogue with himself in which he recorded his inner anguish and solitude. These verses, like those of *Tentativa del hombre infinito,* were considered hermetic and therefore unintelligible to readers unfamiliar with the author's personal circumstances. This time, though, Neruda went out of his way to explain to everyone who would listen, how, alone and cut off from the Hispanic world, he was forced to develop an unusually concentrated mode of expression. Be that as it may, the fact is that he was using Spanish in a new and different way and his readers had relatively little difficulty in accepting it. With punctuation restored, his free verse took on a more controlled cadence. The discourse, although still discontinuous, became almost incantatory in some compositions as sequence after sequence of oneiric imagery was compressed into a new poetic unity. One poem from *Residencia en la tierra* is even titled "Unidad" (Unity) and best illustrates Neruda's concern with this aspect of his expressive system:

Hay algo denso, unido, sentado en el fondo,
repitiendo su número, su señal idéntica.
Cómo se nota que las piedras han tocado el tiempo,
en su fina materia hay olor a edad
y el agua que trae el mar, de sal y sueño.

Me rodea una misma cosa, un solo movimiento:
el peso del mineral, la luz de la piel,
se pegan al sonido de la palabra noche:
la tinta del trigo, del marfil, del llanto,

las cosas de cuero, de madera, de lana,
envejecidas, desteñidas, uniformes,
se unen en torno a mí como paredes.

Trabajo sordamente, girando sobre mí mismo,
como el cuervo sobre la muerte, el cuervo de luto.
Pienso, aislado en lo extenso de las estaciones,
central, rodeado de geografía silenciosa:
una temperatura parcial cae del cielo,
un extremo imperio de confusas unidades
se reúne rodeándome.

There is something dense, unified, seated at the bottom, repeating its number, its redundant signal. How evident is the presence of time on stones, in its delicate matter there is the scent of age and the water the sea brings, salty and dreamy. The same thing encircles me, a single movement: the weight of mineral, the glow of skin, stick to the sound of the word night: the juice of wheat, of ivory, of weeping, things of leather, of wood, of wool, things old, faded, uniform, unite around me like walls. I labor deafly, circling around myself, like the crow over death, the crow of death. I meditate isolated in the length of the seasons, central, surrounded by silent geography: a partisan temperature falls from the sky, a radical empire of confused unities draw together surrounding me.

This silence, this deafness of the final stanza alludes to Neruda's Far East experience and is a key to the hermetic modality of his poetic practice at this time. The role and the posture of the artist is quite changed. The substantiality of the world that surrounds him serves to encase the writer, existentially cutting him off from everything save his own experience.

All poetry rests on certain metaphysical assumptions. The Hispanic Modernists, for example, were anguished over the uncertainty of a meaningful afterlife. Here, Neruda breaks with this fin-de-siècle literary posture and chooses instead to languish in the absolute certainty of universal death. This in fact is the unity to which the title of the poem refers; the unspecifiable substance, the "algo denso" that engulfs all things in an inexorable movement toward death is made concrete in the text. This poem—indeed, all of the compositions of *Residencia en la tierra*—is devastatingly pessimistic.

As the manuscript of the book began to circulate it disconcerted many of Neruda's admirers and friends. The prevailing attitude was that the author of the lusty love poems had changed too much; he was just too young to be so serious, or at least to be taken seriously for being so. Ironically, whereas *Veinte poemas de amor* had been condemned for being too explicit, *Residencia en la tierra* would be considered too closed, too hermetic. Again, Neruda had more than a little difficulty in finding someone who would accept it for publication. And again, he himself was more convinced than ever of his latest work's greatness. In 1928, when he thought he was about to complete the manuscript and some seven years before he was to succeed in finding the right publisher for it, Neruda was certain that *Residencia en la tierra* was to be a masterpiece. He was ultimately correct, but we must remember that he was only twenty-four years old at the time. In this connection there is a most interesting letter from Neruda to an Argentine friend, Héctor Eandi, dated September 8, 1928, in which he confidently, and quite immodestly, speaks of his accomplishment:

> I have just about finished a new book of poems, *Residencia en la tierra,* and you will soon see how I manage to isolate my expression, making it hesitate constantly between risks, and with what a solid and uniform substance I am able to consistently give expression to the same force.

And, a year later, in October 1929:

> I have been thinking about my book of new poems. Is what you tell me possible, that in Buenos Aires something would be paid for them? I am going to tell you though, my greatest interest is to publish in Spain. Argentina seems to me too provincial, Madrid is quite different . . . I have been writing these poems for almost five years now, and as you can see there are very

few, only 19, yet it seems to me that I have attained this one obligatory essense: a style.*

Notwithstanding the book's importance, but perhaps because of the author's unbridled ambitions for it, the publication of *Residencia en la tierra* was delayed for several years. Neruda did not like the kind of criticism his earlier works had received in Chile, and he felt it imperative that he publish his next book in Spain. To that end he appealed to another poet, the Spaniard Rafael Alberti, to find him a publisher there. Unfortunately, Alberti's publisher went bankrupt before bringing out Neruda's book. He then gave the manuscript to someone who promised to publish it in France; but nothing ever came of this project either. As a consequence, in 1933 Neruda himself brought out the book—not in Europe, but with Nascimento, the Chilean publisher who had once been so reluctant to print his love poems. This time, however, it is Neruda who is holding back. Convinced of the greatness of his latest work and intent on eventually publishing it in Spain, he limited the Chilean edition of *Residencia en la tierra* to exactly one hundred copies, just enough to send to the critics and influential men of letters whose enthusiastic commentaries virtually assured its later success by creating advance interest in the work. Thus, in 1935, two years after the private Chilean printing and some seven years after Neruda had first announced the completion of the book, it was at last published in Spain, in the now famous Cruz y Raya edition. By this time Neruda was beginning to be considered something of a force in Hispanic poetry. The hermetic style of expression he had tried out in *Tentativa del hombre infinito* and perfected in *Residencia en la tierra* was soon to spread all over the Spanish-speaking world, beginning the cycle of imitation and emulation that has come to be called Nerudism.

The poet's arrogant confidence in the value of his work, combined with his attempt to engineer a literary success in

* Unpublished letters; quoted in Margarita Aguirre, *Las vidas de Pablo Neruda* (Santiago, Zig-Zag, 1967), pp. 179–183.

Europe, would earn him many enemies. A polemic soon ensued which involved the principal writers of Spain and Chile. Its only literary outcome was a powerfully virulent defense which Neruda belligerently entitled "Aquí estoy" (Here I am). Although the composition was clearly not intended for publication, the poet allowed it to be widely circulated among his friends with the intention that it should eventually reach those against whom it was directed: his compatriots Pablo de Rokha and Vicente Huidobro. The opening strophes suffice to give an idea of the poem's extraordinary scatological power:

> Estoy aquí con mis labios de hierro
> y un ojo en cada mano,
> y con mi corazón completamente,
> y viene el alba, y viene el alba,
> y estoy aquí a pesar
> de perros, a pesar
> de lobos, a pesar
> de pesadillas, a pesar
> de ladillas, a pesar de pesares
> estoy lleno de lágrimas y amapolas cortadas,
> y pálidas palomas de energía,
> y con todos los dientes y los dedos escribo,
> y con todas las materias del mar,
> con todas las materias del corazón escribo.
>
> Cabrones!
> Hijos de putas!
> Hoy ni mañana
> ni jamás
> acabaréis conmigo!
> Tengo llenos de pétalos los testículos,
> tengo lleno de pájaros el pelo,
> tengo poesía y vapores,
> cementerios y casas,
> gente que se ahoga,
> incendios,
> en mis "Veinte poemas,"
> en mis semanas, en mis caballerías,

y me cago en la puta que os malparió,
derokas, patíbulos,
Vidobras . . .*

⌈Here I am with my lips of iron and one eye in each hand, and
with my heart completely, and dawn comes, and dawn comes,
and I am here in spite of dogs, in spite of wolves, in spite of
nightmares, in spite of lice, in spite of spites I have had enough
of tears of cut poppies, and palled lovebirds of energy, and with
all my teeth and my fingers do I write, and with all the matter of
the sea, with all the matter of my heart do I write.⌋   Bastards!
Sons of whores! Neither today nor tomorrow not ever will you
be finished with me! Filled with petals are my testicles, filled
with birds is my hair, I have poetry and steam, cemeteries and
houses, people who gasp, fires, in my "Twenty poems," in my
weeks, in my adventures, and I shit on the whore who gave birth
to you, de Rokhas, gallows, snakey Huidobros . . .

The diction is unmistakably that of *Residencia en la tierra*. As
in "Unidad," the poet makes concrete an abstract reality, postu-
lating an organic unity that exists only through the material
imagery of the poetry. Although time has rendered meaningless
the original circumstances of the polemic with Huidobro and
de Rokha, the literary power of Neruda's art remains.

Curiously enough, *Residencia en la tierra,* the text that set
off this controversy and the one that has had the most lasting
impact on Hispanic poetry in our time, is the very same text that
Neruda himself would one day deem unpublishable. In 1949,
not long after joining the Communist Party, he denounced the
poems of *Residencia en la tierra* and, for a time at least, even
prevented their being republished and translated. In an inter-
view at that time, he explained the reason for his changed
attitude: "Contemplating them now, I consider the poems of
Residencia en la tierra to be harmful. These poems should not

---

* Unpublished poem of some 230 lines. Typescript, dated April 2,
1935, in the Department of Special Collections, SUNY Library, Stony
Brook, New York.

be read by the youth of our countries. They are poems which are saturated with pessimism and an atrocious anguish. They do not support life, they support death."* Neruda had come to subscribe to the idea that poetry was to have a social function. In this committed view, art and literature were to be essential rather than existential; poetry was not to be the intimate record of an individual existence, it was to speak out to all men. Its purpose was not to be confessional, but missionary; not to reveal, but to persuade. Predictably, this new and somewhat orthodox kind of writing turned out to be most controversial and, for a while, Neruda was practically unpublishable in his own country. In fact, in the late 1940s, as Chile entered the Cold War with its own version of McCarthyism, he was blacklisted so as to prevent the publication and distribution of his most recent work of social commitment.

Canto general, the majestic epic of America whose thousands of verses range from the mystic exaltation of the "Alturas de Macchu Picchu" (Heights of Macchu Picchu) to the political condemnation of the Anaconda Mining Company, was first published in Mexico in 1950. Banned at the time in Chile, and diffused there through clandestine editions by the Communist Party, its subversive quality helped to assure its success. Again, it is the controversial aspect of Neruda and his work that points up the dynamic nature of the changes in his poetry.

In a sense the controversy surrounding each major work makes it relatively easy to identify its uniqueness, but it does not satisfactorily explain the mechanism of change. To do this, the genesis of each major new work must be studied. In this way it is possible to see that the poetry of social commitment so troublesome to some readers in 1950 was taking shape long before the publication of *Canto general.* One of the volume's lead poems, "Alturas de Macchu Picchu," was published separately in 1946, even before the political poetry of *Tercera resi-*

---

* Alfredo Cardona Peña "Pablo Neruda: breve historia de sus libros," *Cuadernos Americanos,* 9:6 (November–December 1950).

dencia (The Third Residence) raised a few eyebrows in 1947. With regard to this relatively unstudied volume, it is interesting that the critical hostility to some of its poems surfaced quite early—in 1937 in Spain and in 1942 in Mexico.

During the Second World War Neruda wrote and made public a poem that was to set off an international incident. At the height of the war he took a strong political stand in a poem to Stalingrad. In September 1942, when things were still going badly for the United States and its ally, Russia, Neruda was in Mexico City. He there gave a public reading of his poems, one of which was called "Canto a Stalingrado" (Song to Stalingrad), a spirited ballad to the defenders of the Russian city then under seige by the invading Nazis. The poem made the audience and the official critics uncomfortable. Mexico had not then declared war on the Axis and there were many complaints that Neruda was "partisan." His response was immediate. He authorized the poem to Stalingrad to be reproduced as a poster; a few days later it was plastered all over the streets of Mexico. For many this was an unpardonable provocation. He was forced to leave the country, but before his departure he composed yet another political poem on the same subject, the "Nuevo canto de amor a Stalingrado" (New Song of Love to Stalingrad)—a poem even more powerful and abrasive than the first. In the opening stanzas of this composition it is not difficult to appreciate the art of Neruda's political poetry:

> Yo escribí sobre el tiempo y sobre el agua
> describí el luto y su metal morado,
> yo escribí sobre el cielo y la manzana,
>   ahora escribo sobre Stalingrado.
>
> Ya la novia guardó con su pañuelo
> el rayo de mi amor enamorado,
> ahora mi corazón está en el suelo,
>   en el humo y la luz de Stalingrado.
>
> Yo toqué con mis manos la camisa
> del crepúsculo azul y derrotado:

ahora toco el alba de la vida
   naciendo con el sol de Stalingrado.

Yo sé que el viejo joven transitorio
de pluma, como un cisne encuadernado,
desencuaderna su dolor notorio
       por mi grito de amor a Stalingrado.

Yo pongo el alma mía donde quiero.
Y no me nutro de papel cansado,
adobado de tinta y de tintero.
       Nací para cantar a Stalingrado.

I wrote about weather and water I described mourning and its purple character, I wrote about the sky and the apple, now I write about Stalingrad.   The bride already put away with her handkerchief the lightning bolt of my loving love, now my heart is on the ground, in the smoke and light of Stalingrad.   I touched with my hands the shirt of the blue and defeated dusk: now I touch the dawn of life rising with the sun of Stalingrad.   I know that the old youth of changing plumage, like the bookbound swan, unbinds his proverbial grief because of my love cry to Stalingrad.   I put my heart where I please. I do not feed on exhausted paper, basted with ink and with the inkpot. I was born to sing to Stalingrad.

Obviously, Neruda has again altered his expressive system. This is not the hermetic style of *Residencia en la tierra*. There is a disciplined use of rhyme and meter. There is also a change in vocabulary and diction: the language is simple and elevated; the syntax is clear and straightforward. The poet, conscious of his new public responsibility, is no longer speaking and writing as though to himself; he is writing to persuade the reader.

This change in form and style, although radical, is not arbitrary. Neruda's poetry consistently finds its unity in his personal experience. The erotic exaltations of his youth, the somber introspections of his lonely period in the Far East, the deep feeling of social commitment after the Spanish Civil War are not mere stages. Rather, they are part of a continuum in which the author, moving through time and space, experiences the world from a constantly changing perspective and, true artist that he is, his expressive system evolves accordingly. Critics condemned to evaluating the new by measuring it with the old are perpetually one step behind the real creative artist. As a consequence, Neruda's newest poetry has often been judged negatively in the inadequate context of the aesthetic system of his previous work.

More recently, his cultivation of a lighter and more humorous verse angered not only the critics who preferred the baroque introspectiveness of his earlier poems but also disappointed those who admired his serious writing of social commitment. The fact is that with the *Odas elementales* (Elemental Odes), published in 1954, Neruda once again made a radical change in his poetry, surprising his admirers and detractors alike, and winning over a whole new sector of readers with a collection of elegantly serendipitous verses praising the seemingly "unpoetic" things of daily life, such as artichokes, or even an onion, as in the "Oda a la cebolla" (Ode to an Onion):

> Cebolla,
> luminosa redoma,
> pétalo a pétalo
> se formó tu hermosura,
> escamas de cristal te acrecentaron
> y en el secreto de la tierra oscura
> se redondeó tu vientre de rocío.
> Bajo la tierra
> fue el milagro
> y cuando apareció
> tu torpe tallo verde,
> y nacieron
> tus hojas como espadas en el huerto
> la tierra acumuló su poderío
> mostrando tu desnuda transparencia . . .

Onion, luminous ball, petal by petal your beauty was formed, scales of crystal grew on you and in the secret of the dark earth your belly was rounded by the dew. Underground the miracle happened and when appeared your awkward green stem, and were born your leaves like swords in the garden the earth accumulated its power showing your transparent nudity ...

The poem acts as a kind of magnifying lens for the reader, helping him to see the importance of humble things. Beauty is found in the ordinary object, just as poetry is to be found in ordinary speech.

In later books, Neruda went even farther in this direction; after 1958 he turned almost completely to conversational poetry, to what in Spanish has since come to be called "la poesía de lo cotidiano" (the poetry of everyday life). In his first book of such verse, appropriately titled *Estravagario*, extravagant things, Neruda took a derisively mocking midlife look at himself, his poetry, and his critics. One result was "El miedo" (Fear):

Todos me piden que dé saltos,
que tonifique y que futbole,
que corra, que nade y que vuele.
Muy bien.

Todos me aconsejan reposo,
todos me destinan doctores,
mirándome de cierta manera.
Qué pasa?

Todos me aconsejan que viaje,
que entre y que salga, que no viaje,
que me muera y que no me muera.
No importa.

Todos ven las dificultades
de mis vísceras sorprendidas
por radioterribles retratos.
No estoy de acuerdo.

Todos pican mi poesía
con invencibles tenedores
buscando, sin duda, una mosca.
Tengo miedo.

15

Tengo miedo de todo el mundo,
del agua fría, de la muerte.
Soy como todos los mortales,
inaplazable.

Por eso en estos cortos días
no voy a tomarlos en cuenta,
voy a abrirme y voy a encerrarme
con mi más pérfido enemigo,
Pablo Neruda.

Everyone asks me to skip, to tone up and to play football, to run, to swim and to fly. Fine.   Everyone counsels me to rest, everyone sends me doctors, looking at me a certain way. What is happening?   Everyone counsels me to travel, to enter and to leave, not to travel, to drop dead and not to die. It doesn't matter.   Everyone sees the difficulties of my insides surprised by terrible x-rays. I do not agree.   Everyone picks at my poetry with inconquerable forks looking, undoubtedly, for a fly. I am afraid.   I am afraid of everyone, of cold water, of death. I am like all mortals, undelayable.   Therefore in these short days I am not going to pay any attention to them, I am going to open myself up and close myself in with my most perfidious enemy, Pablo Neruda.

Here is fear, not of himself but of the institution he had become. A little like Borges in his celebrated monologue "Borges and I."

Looking back on the few poems highlighted in this introductory chapter, it is clear that Neruda's work does not fit into a simple trajectory. The pattern of development is more complex; it is a pattern in which the only constant element seems, almost paradoxically, to be change itself. For this reason, in the pages that follow, I shall be focusing attention on the dynamic process of this change through an examination of the several distinct poetics of Pablo Neruda as manifested in his major works, the works that, coincidentally, have come to signal more than a few of the epochal developments in Hispanic poetry over the past half-century.

In Temuco, 1919

At the time of *Crepusculario*
(dedicated to Aliro Oyarzún,
1923)

At the time of the Love Poetry,
1924

Neruda surrounded by the Chilean avant-garde, about 1925

A literary banquet, 1924

Detail showing Neruda at a literary banquet

2. Love Poetry

Veinte poemas de amor y una canción desesperada

> I undertook the greatest departure from myself:
> creation, wanting to illuminate words.
>
> *1924*

Veinte poemas de amor y una canción desesperada, Neruda's best known and most widely distributed work today, was also his most personal and, for a time at least, his most controversial. Originally printed in a small edition of probably no more than five hundred copies in Santiago de Chile in 1924, by 1961 its international sales in Spanish alone had passed the million mark. It remains a best-seller to this day; and in English its enigmatic poems of love have been translated, and retranslated, by Tarn, Walsh, and Merwin, among others. Yet the initial reaction of readers and critics was not so positive: the erotic subject was once judged offensive. The problem at the time was that Neruda poetized not love, but sex. Or so it seemed. In fact, the original title he had proposed for the book was almost clinical in its precision: "Poemas de una mujer y un hombre" (Poems of a Woman and a Man). Between the public taste of today and that of 1924 there is a considerable difference. Therefore, before attempting to appraise the literary qualities of the work, we must take into account its initial shock value, its sensationalism in its original cultural context.

We know now that some of the love poems had been rejected by the literary journals of the time and that the book itself was turned down by Nascimento, then Chile's most successful publisher. We also know that such disapproval, according to the bohemian standard of the time, might be advantageously provoked: rejection by the establishment as a proof of artistic originality. Yet Neruda, despite his decadent posturing, did not provoke nor exploit disapproval of his love poetry. On the contrary, he privately, and determinedly, solicited support for its publication from Santiago's principal literary figures; the critic Alone, the poet Pedro Prado, and the novelist Eduardo Barrios.

Neruda, then only nineteen, was confident of the value of his new poetry and anxious to get it into print. His haste and anxiety might seem difficult to understand, for this was not his first incursion into literature. He had been writing rather regularly for *Claridad,* the anarchist publication of the Chilean student federation (modeled after *Clarté,* the internationalist review of Henri Barbusse and Anatole France), and had even enjoyed a certain succès d'estime with the publication of *Crepusculario,* a collection of his youthful verses (1919–1923). When his love poems were rejected he was just beginning to establish himself in Santiago as a local figure of note. And, when they were finally published he emerged on the literary scene as a major new poetic voice in the Spanish language. How did this come about?

The biographical data concerning Neruda's formative years is not terribly revealing. Born in Parral in 1904, as Neftalí Ricardo Reyes Basoalto, the son of a railroad worker, and raised in Temuco, a rough-and-tumble frontier town in the south of Chile, he arrived in Santiago in 1921 as a scholarship student to specialize in French at the Instituto Pedagógico of the University of Chile. His goal was modest: to become a secondary schoolteacher. Like his "maestra rural," Lucila Godoy Alcayaga, later known to literature as Gabriela Mistral, he adopted a pen name, Pablo Neruda, as much to mask his humble origins as to establish a literary identity for himself. Understandably, his early attempts at literature were for the most part bookish and imitative, respecting the refined aesthetic norms of Hispanic Modernism.

Later, as a provincial in the capital, he continued in this same vein, seeming somewhat more affected by the nightlife of metropolitan Santiago than by the formal study of French literature. His poetry began to reflect this combined cultural experience in an uneven yet routine sort of way. And *Crepusculario,* his first book, published with woodcuts by his cohorts at *Claridad* in 1923, was a curious pastiche of compositions as predictable as "El nuevo soneto a Helena" (New Sonnet to Hélène), an elegant imitation of Ronsard, and as unusual as "Maestranzas de noche" (Arsenal Workers on the Night Shift) and "Barrio sin luz" (Neighborhood without Electricity), poems which seem to have been conceived as urban nocturnes. "Final," the volume's closing piece, is both ecstatic and contrite, containing perhaps an intentional apology for this strange admixture:

> Fueron creadas por mí estas palabras
> con sangre mía, con dolores míos
> fueron creadas!
> Yo lo comprendo, amigos, yo lo comprendo todo.
> Se mezclaron voces ajenas a las mías,
> yo lo comprendo, amigos!

> These words were created by me with my blood, with my pains
> they were created! And I understand, friends, I understand it all.
> Strange voices got mixed in with mine, and I understand it,
> friends!

To be sure, there are some excellent compositions in *Crepusculario,* and many have been anthologized, but the book, like its title, belongs to another era, and in the avant-garde literary context of the 1920s it is not distinguished. However, its publication must have been purgative, for, once in print, Neruda seems to have been able to set it behind him and to give himself over almost entirely to a new kind of writing, an apparently spontaneous lyricism. It is with his love poems that he finds a uniquely personal voice. As early as February 1923 we find him writing to Alone, the literary critic of *Zig Zag*, to tell him that he is hard at work on a new book and to ask him to use his influence with the journal's editor, Carlos Acuña, so as to publish "Vaso de amor" (Goblet of Love), a composition which later, and with some revisions, would reappear as one of the twenty poems of love (Poem XII). Noteworthy at this time is Neruda's pronounced assurance with regard to this work:

> I am sending you four poems now. Three I send to you, so that you can read them, only for that. The other, which is called "Vaso de amor," is the one I would like to be published. It is a question of pride, because Sr. Carlos Acuña didn't want to publish them and nothing of mine will come out in the magazine, with my consent, until these verses appear there. Please, Alone, reply to me if you receive this and tell me how you feel about it. They are from my book *Poemas de una mujer y un hombre**

And later, when Jorge Nascimento rejected the manuscript for the book, Neruda would write to Pedro Prado with the same assurance, smarting only over the publisher's foolhardy mistake: "Le pesará, les pesará a todos." Prado interceded and Nascimento did publish the book. The magazine *Zig Zag* also published the poem. The important thing to note with regard to the poet's attitude toward his work at this point is the absolute certainty he has of its quality.

Once the little book of love poems appeared and the hostility of some readers and critics began to manifest itself, Neruda publicly came to its defense, equating its integrity with his own. In an open letter to Santiago's *La Nación* (August 20, 1924), he made a kind of exegesis, pompously and with romantic exag-

---

* The letter has been published by Alone (Hernán Díaz Arrieta) in his *Cuatro grandes de la literatura chilena* (Santiago: Zig-Zag, 1962), p. 220.

geration referring to the difficult struggle with himself that was necessary to bring the project to completion:

> I undertook the greatest departure from myself: creation, wanting to illuminate words. Ten years of solitary labor, exactly half my life, have made diverse rhythms and contrary currents succeed one another in my expression. Grasping them, weaving them together, without ever finding the endurable element, because it does not exist, there you have my *Veinte poemas de amor y una canción desesperada*. Disperse as thought in its elusive variation, happy and sad, I have made these poems and I have suffered much in making them.

The wounded artists seeks the compassion of his public. But no longer does he apologize for the inadequacies of his art, as in *Crepusculario*. Confident of his achievement, he stresses the difficulty of his craft and the authenticity of his effort. Gone is the Modernist concern with formal perfection. What counts now is the result, the sensation of pure lyricism he was able to achieve in these poems of love.

Traditionally love poetry has equated woman with nature. Neruda took this established mode of comparison and raised it to a cosmic level, making woman into a veritable force of the universe. By way of illustration, let us examine the mechanism of the explicit metaphor of the introductory poem, a metaphor as powerful today as it was fifty years ago when it served to introduce the theme of the book and to set its tone:

> Cuerpo de mujer, blancas colinas, muslos blancos,
> te pareces al mundo en tu actitud de entrega.

> Body of woman, white hills, white thighs, you look like the world in your attitude of giving.

Noteworthy here is the use of the alexandrine, a traditional verse form, to modulate the otherwise understated metaphor. The alexandrine, a fourteen-syllable line and the standard vehicle of serious narrative poetry in Spanish since the later Middle Ages, had been given new life by the Modernists who found that by changing the distribution of measured accents the stately verse could be made quite supple. Neruda combines medieval tradition and Modernist innovations to give this couplet its persuasive dignity. The first line is melodic and iterative, its accentuated pauses dividing the verse in three parts: "Cuerpo de mujer / blancas colinas / muslos blancos." The next line is more traditional, its natural separation into hemistiches being used to form an equation, balanced and assertive: "te pareces al mundo / en tu actitud de entrega." This line somewhat weightily restates the idea only barely suggested at the outset: that woman is, like the world, bounteously available. The resultant metaphor, once completed, is far more powerful than the simile on which it is based because it is the reader who must imaginatively supply the link between the two things being related: woman's body and the world. In the first line it is the emphasized repetition of the adjective *blanco* which serves syntactically to relate thighs to hills and forces the reader to complete the metaphor, an imagistic transference which is, in truth, based not on the stated similarity of the color white, but the implied similarity of shape. A proposition that would be ridiculously hyperbolic were it expressed directly. Neruda is short-circuiting words and meanings in order to create a highly charged contemporary *stil nuovo* in these modern poems of love.

In Poem XIII the discontinuous and irregular line of free verse combined with ellipsis is skillfully used to charge the strophe with a sense of action:

> He ido marcando con cruces de fuego
> el atlas blanco de tu cuerpo.
> Mi boca era una araña que cruzaba escondiéndose.
> En ti, detrás de ti, temerosa, sedienta.

> I have gone along marking with crosses of fire the white atlas of your body. My mouth was a spider that would move about hiding itself. In you, behind you, fearful, thirsty.

Again it is the special and strategic use of an ordinary word, the adjective *blanco,* which serves to place this poem's imagery of action in the same cosmic dimension as "Cuerpo de mujer."

Obviously the power of Neruda's love poetry does not derive from the subject alone. Although the book's explicitness may have shocked the sensibility of some readers in 1924, in Neruda's more immediate cultural context, the anarchist milieu of the militant student groups of the twenties, a frank attitude toward sex was the norm rather than the exception. *Claridad* was then championing a free love movement of sorts, and in July 1921, in an article aptly titled "Sexo" (Sex), Neruda himself unambiguously dealt with the issue:

> He is strong and young. The ardent flash of sex courses through his veins in electric shocks. The pleasure has now been discovered and it attracts him as the simplest and most marvelous thing that he has ever been shown. Earlier he was taught to hide the filthiness of his groin and his child's face would wrinkle up in an unconscious query. Later a friend revealed to him the secret. And the solitary pleasure went on to corrupt the purity of his soul and to open him up to pleasures hitherto unknown.
>
> But that time has passed. Now, strong and young, he hunts for an object in which to empty out his cup of youth. He is the animal that simply hunts for an outlet for his natural potency. He is the male and life should supply him with the female in whom he can find satisfaction.

The article goes on to condemn the system of moral values which serve only to impede the satisfaction of a drive as natural as sex.

The free love movement was basically male chauvinist; it hailed the woman as sex-object while piously condemning as bourgeois certain social conventions, especially marriage and chastity. While still a teenager, Neruda gave poetic form to this blatant new sexism in "Canción de adiós" (Goodby Song), a poem first published in *Claridad* in August 1922. An anticipation of the much anthologized "Farewell," this poem is openly addressed to woman as sex-object. Pregnant, she is destined to be abandoned:

> Fui tuyo, fuiste mía. ¿Qué más? Juntos hicimos
> un recodo en la ruta donde el amor pasó.
>
> Fui tuyo, fuiste mía. Tú serás del que te ame,
> del que corte en tu huerto lo que he sembrado yo.
>
> Yo me voy. Estoy triste: pero siempre estoy triste.
> Vengo desde tus brazos. No sé hacia dónde voy.
>
> Desde tu corazón me dice adiós un niño.
> Y yo le digo adiós.

> I was yours, you were mine. What more? Together we made a bend in the road where love passed by.   I was yours, you were mine. You will belong to the one who loves you, the one who reaps in your garden what I have planted.   I am leaving. I am sad: but I am always sad. I come from your arms. I don't know where I am going.   From your heart a child says goodbye to me. And I say goodbye to him.

This poem, in spite of its prosaic diction and its heartless sentimentality, was a favorite of the students of Neruda's generation. Its refrain "Amo el amor de los marineros que besan y se van" (I love the love of the sailors who kiss and depart) has even passed into Chilean popular culture with the repeated force of a maxim.

At this juncture it is well to ask if the outspoken references to sex in *Veinte poemas de amor* were really so revolutionary after all. They were and they were not. The deciding factor of course is in the readership, the public to whom they were directed. Neruda did not care to publish his first love poem, "Vaso de amor," in the anarchist review to which he had ready access, but in *Zig Zag,* a more prestigious family magazine. By the same token he wanted the book to be brought out not by his bohemian friends at *Claridad,* who had earlier printed

Crepusculario, but by Nascimento, Chile's most respectable publishing house. Neruda was ambitious; he was looking for a wider audience and recognition. He hoped to reach the readers of traditional poetry, readers who, although initially disturbed by his theme, might ultimately prove responsive to his style. His ambition was not unrealistic, for this is exactly what did happen with Alone and Pedro Prado. In their case, the quality of Neruda's poetry did overcome their original distaste for his treatment of sex. And so it was with others once the book was in print. Neruda, at twenty, seems to have had an intuitive feel for the "selling" of his literature.

From succès d'estime with *Crepusculario* in 1923 to succès de scandale with the love poems in 1924, in somewhat less than a year the attention of readers and critics had been effectively focused on the young provincial and his works. Lionized in formerly hostile Santiago, he soon became the spokesman for the nascent Chilean avant-garde and his poetry was much admired and widely imitated. But it was not studied. In fact, the art of Neruda's love poetry, until quite recently, has not been the object of serious analysis. Critics have preferred to dwell on the so-called question of its sources,* or to speculate on the identity of the women who may have inspired each poem. Given the lyric intensity of the poetry, such speculation was perhaps not unwarranted. However, over the years Neruda consistently discouraged any and all biographic interpretations. Not until 1954, in a speech at the University of Chile some thirty years after the first publication of the love poems, did the poet publicly refer to their basis in his personal life:

* The case of Poem XVI is notorious. In the 1930s, when Neruda achieved international recognition with the publication of *Residencia en la tierra,* much was made in Chile over the fact that this composition closely resembled a poem by Tagore. Accordingly, Neruda added a note to the 1938 edition: "Poem XVI is, principally, a paraphrase of a poem of Rabindranath Tagore, in *El jardinero.* This has always been publicly and publishedly known. Those resentful souls who have tried to take advantage of this circumstance during my absence, have fallen into the oblivion they deserve faced by the enduring vitality of this adolescent book."

I have promised you an explanation of each of my poems of love. I had forgotten that many years have passed. It is not that I have forgotten anyone, rather what would be gained with the names I could give you . . . There are two fundamental loves in this book, that which filled my adolescence as a provincial and that which awaited me later in the labyrinth of Santiago. In *Veinte poemas* . . . they are conjoined from one page to another, so that in one place there is a flash of the forest and in another a backdrop of sweet darkness.*

And some eight years later, as Neruda was approaching sixty, he went on to clarify somewhat the evasiveness of the earlier explanation, calling the country girl *Marisol* and the city girl *Marisombra:*

> *Marisol* is the idyll of the enchanted province, with immense evening stars and dark eyes like the wet sky of Temuco. She figures, with her happiness and her lively legend, in nearly all the pages surrounded by the waters of the port and by the half moon over the mountains. *Marisombra* is the student of the capital. Gray cap, soft eyes, the constant scent of honeysuckle of our nomadic student love. The physical calm of passionate encounters in the hideaways of the city.†

Supposedly, poems III, IV, VI, VIII, IX, X, XII, XVI, XIX, and XX refer to *Marisol,* and the remaining ten to *Marisombra.* The only trouble with this authorial classification is that it does not correspond to the internal evidence of the poetry. Critics, quite naturally, were quick to point out certain discrepancies. Poem VI, for example:

> This poem presents a curious problem. Because Neruda has identified it as belonging to the Temuco cycle but at the same

---

* Unpublished speech; quoted in Aguirre, *Las vidas de Pablo Neruda,* p. 142.

† "Memorias y recuerdos de Pablo Neruda," *O Cruzeiro Internacional* (Rio de Janeiro), February 1, 1962, p. 64.

time, on speaking of *Marisombra,* the girl from Santiago, he has referred to her gray cap (these are poems from the era of caps); perhaps the poet's memory has placed the cap of one on the head of the other; perhaps (hypothesis not to be disdained), the poems have not been created in such a symmetrically separate way: the two muses of flesh and blood can be fused at times into one, composed of sounds and visions.*

It would seem that with the death of the poet in 1973 the real identities of the women would remain forever unknown. But in 1974 an edition of some purloined love letters from Neruda's student days in Santiago was published in Spain. These letters, addressed to Albertina Rosa Azócar Soto, a coed at the Instituto Pedagógico, clarify the biographic circumstances of the poetry. By all evidence, Neruda and Albertina had an impassioned affair, which for economic and professional reasons could not be consummated in marriage, a kind of working-class neoromantic "impossible love." Albertina, the student from Santiago, is the girl of the gray cap. We now know that it was to her that Neruda wrote in September 1923:

> Little one, yesterday you should have received a journal, and in it a poem on the absent one. (You are the absent one.) Did you like it, little one? Are you convinced that I remember you? On the other hand, you. In ten days, one letter. Me, spread out on the grass, in the evenings, I dream of your gray cap, of your eyes that I love, of you.†

Intriguing as the personal details of these letters may be, they tell us woefully little about the composition of the poetry. In Poem VI, for example, what interests us is not whether the gray cap belonged to Albertina, but the use the poet made of it. The poem's imagery is autonomous. The cap, the identity of whose

* Emir Rodríguez Monegal, *El viajero inmóvil* (Buenos Aires, Losada, 1966), p. 49.

† *Cartas de amor de Pablo Neruda* (Madrid, Rodas, 1974), p. 202.

owner has inordinately concerned several generations of Neruda scholars, is never identified in the poem as belonging to anyone in particular; its function is to personify the absent lover and thus to make the expressed feeling of that absence more intense:

> Te recuerdo como eras en el último otoño.
> Eras la boina gris y el corazón en calma.
> . . . .
> Siento viajar tus ojos y es distante el otoño:
> boina gris, voz de pájaro y corazón de casa.

> I remember you as you were last Autumn. You were the gray cap and the heart at peace . . . I feel your eyes traveling and Autumn is far away: gray cap, voice of a bird and heart of home.

Neruda employs a concentrated literary language here. In the first pair of verses the repetition of the same verb form ("eras") in a distinct context establishes the comparison, completing the metaphor in a way that is both subtle and direct. In the second pair the pain of loss is evoked by references not to the absent lover but to the memory of her presence. Again, the condensed language allows many subtle transfers of meaning. Time and space are mixed, establishing the feeling of remoteness, of a distancing process (*"Siento viajar tus ojos y es distante el otoño"*). Albertina Rosa, the subject, has been transformed into the object of poetry. The love poems, rhetorically addressed to her, are potentiated in the mind of the reader who seems categorically excluded from the text. The recently published love letters verify what is already evident in the poetry itself—its hermetic modality. Lyric apostrophes addressed not to the reader but to someone absent, the voice of the speaker in each poem of love is conscious of the discourse and of its incompleteness.

Each composition is a kind of monologue in which the poet speaks as though to himself. It might be more accurate to say that the discursive situation is that of a man alone, writing and revising, correcting his expression. The opening lines of the last of the twenty love poems best define this situation:

> Puedo escribir los versos más tristes esta noche.
>
> Escribir, por ejemplo: "La noche está estrellada,
> y tiritan, azules, los astros, a lo lejos."

> I can write the saddest verses tonight.   Write, for example:
> "The night is starry, and the stars twinkle, blue, in the distance."

The example of what one might write, placed in quotation marks here as in the original, is a recognizable commonplace, cited in the poem only for its banality. It is all too easy for thought to be channeled into a conventional "literary" formula: the twinkling of the stars. The real subject of this composition is not the speaker's stated sadness but the disparity between this sentiment and the words he can summon to express what he feels. The poem, with thirty-two lines the longest of the twenty, is organized as a series of statements of sadness and frustrated attempts to deal with this feeling poetically. The initial line, a declaration of intention and even of capability—"Puedo escribir . . ."—is repeated several times and is on each occasion the point of departure for a new and revised attempt to poetize the author's changing sentiment:

> *Puedo escribir los versos más tristes esta noche.*
>
> Escribir, por ejemplo: "La noche está estrellada,
> y tiritan, azules, los astros, a lo lejos."
>
> El viento de la noche gira en el cielo y canta.
>
> (5) *Puedo escribir los versos más tristes esta noche.*
> *Yo la quise, y a veces ella también me quiso.*
>
> En las noches como ésta la tuve entre mis brazos.
> La besé tantas veces bajo el cielo infinito.
>
> *Ella me quiso, a veces yo también la quería.*
>
> (10) Cómo no haber amado sus grandes ojos fijos.

Puedo escribir los versos más tristes esta noche.
Pensar que no la tengo. Sentir que la he perdido.

Oír la noche inmensa, más inmensa sin ella.
Y el verso cae al alma como al pasto el rocío.

(15)   Qué importa que mi amor no pudiera guardarla.
La noche está estrellada y ella no está conmigo.

Eso es todo. A lo lejos alguien canta. A lo lejos.
Mi alma no se contenta con haberla perdido.

Como para acercarla mi mirada la busca.
(20)   Mi corazón la busca, y ella no está conmigo.

La misma noche que hace blanquear los mismos árboles.
Nosotros, los de entonces, ya no somos los mismos.

Ya no la quiero, es cierto, pero cuánto la quise.
Mi voz buscaba el viento para tocar su oído.

(25)   De otro. Será de otro. Como antes de mis besos.
Su voz, su cuerpo claro. Sus ojos infinitos.

Ya no la quiero, es cierto, pero tal vez la quiero.
Es tan corto el amor, y es tan largo el olvido.

Porque en noches como ésta la tuve entre mis brazos,
(30)   mi alma no se contenta con haberla perdido.

Aunque éste sea el último dolor que ella me causa,
y éstos sean los últimos versos que yo le escribo.

(Emphasis mine)

I can write the saddest verses tonight.   Write, for example: "The night is starry, and the stars twinkle, blue, in the distance."   The wind of the night whirls in the sky and sings.   I can write the saddest verses tonight. I loved her, and sometimes she loved me too.   On nights like this I had her in my arms. I kissed her so many times under the infinite sky.   She loved me, at times I used to love her. How not to love her large fixed eyes.   I can write the saddest verses tonight. To think that I do not have her. To feel that I have lost her.   To hear the immense night, more immense without her. And the verse falls on the soul like the dew on the grass.   What does it matter that my love could not keep her.

The night is starry and she is not with me.   That is all. In the
distance someone sings. In the distance. My soul is not content
with having lost her.   As though to make her near my glance
searches her out. My heart searches for her, and she is not with
me.   The same night that makes the same trees white. We,
those of that time, we are no longer the same.   I no longer
love her, it is true, but how much I once loved her. My voice
searched the wind to reach her ear.   Someone else's. She'll be-
long to another. As before my kisses. Her voice, her clear body.
Her infinite eyes.   I do not love her, it is true, but perhaps I do
love her. Love is so short and oblivion is so long.   Because on
nights like this I had her in my arms, my soul is not content with
having lost her.   Even though this may be the last pain she
causes me, and these may be the last verses I write to her.

In my transcription of the poem certain lines have been itali-
cized in order to emphasize the temporal progression and the
speaker's shifting sentiments: from the anguished present of
composition ("Puedo escribir") to the remote past of the pret-
erite tense (line 6: "Yo la *quise,* y a veces ella también me
quiso"); the subsequent opening up of the past introduced by
the imperfect tense (line 9: "Ella me quiso, a veces yo también la
quería"); a return to the sincerity of the present with a less
"poetized" restatement of the initially cited situation (line 16;
"La noche está estrellada y ella no está conmigo"); an imagina-
tive and pained glimpse into the future of probability (line 25:
"De otro. Será de otro. Como antes de mis besos"); and, finally,
a return to the present of composition, the anguished and termi-
nal situation of the writer of the poem:

> Porque en noches como ésta la tuve entre mis brazos,
> mi alma no se contenta con haberla perdido.
>
> Aunque éste sea el último dolor que ella me causa,
> y éstos sean los últimos versos que yo le escribo.

The poem's effectiveness, the reader's empathy with the sincer-
ity of the poetic voice, derives from the fact that this is a com-

position unlike any other. Neruda has employed here a rhetoric that is not conventionally poetic. The staggered repetitions, the prosaic syntax, the irregularity of the temporal exposition are distinctive features to be sure, but features not normally found in "good poetry." Neruda was writing against this tradition, and this was his book's charm and its challenge for the reader of the time.

Reading this entire volume today in the light of what we now know of the circumstances under which it was originally written, it is easy to perceive its overall structure. Poem XX closes a series of unsuccessful attempts to communicate with the loved one; it is followed, significantly enough, by "La canción deses-perada" (Song of Desperation), a final recognition of failure. It is as though each composition contained a separate and special effort to express the same sentiment of sadness and absence. Only the form of each poem is different. Elegant alexandrines, fixed and unfixed strophic patterns, assonance, consonance, and suppressed rhyme are all used to treat the constant theme of love and loss. This diversity of form and unity of theme and, ultimately, of style combine to communicate a quality much exalted by Romanticism, yet all too often absent from even the best Romantic poetry: the quality of sincerity. Like twenty failed attempts to express the same sentiments, closed by a final cry of desperation, Neruda's book was calculated to affect its reader, any reader, us or Albertina.

For many readers in 1924 it was too explicit; for others it was too obscure. Its explicitness, as we have already observed, is relative, but its obscurity less so, since it derives directly from the method of Neruda's expression as well as the moment of experience he chooses to poetize. The moment of introspection, when the inner self speaks directly to the mind, it is this moment that Neruda treats in his love poetry. The moment when the unarticulated flow of thought has still not been exteriorized. Poem XVII contains a kind of *ars poetica* of the post-Freudian age:

Pensando, enredando sombras en la profunda soledad.
. . . .
Pensando, soltando pájaros, desvaneciendo imágenes,
enterrando lámparas.

Thinking, trapping shadows in the profound solitude . . . Think-
ing, letting birds loose, undoing images, burying lamps.

The concentrated intensity of such disarticulation makes these
poems speak with the same unusual power to the reader of
today as to the reader of 1924. The modern reader, no longer
shocked by the sexuality of the poetry, is moved by the con-
fessional intimacy of the emotions that are being exteriorized.

Poem V directly treats the theme of communication and even
elaborates somewhat on the Becquerian formula of whispered
poetry, of a coded expression of intimacy denuded of literary
rhetoric:

Para que tú me oigas
mis palabras se adelgazan a veces
como las huellas de las gaviotas en las playas.
. . . .
Y las miro lejanas mis palabras.
Más que mías son tuyas.
Van trepando en mi viejo dolor como las yedras.
. . . .
Antes que tú poblaron la soledad que ocupas,
y están acostumbradas más que tú a mi tristeza.

Ahora quiero que digan lo que quiero decirte
para que tú me oigas como quiero que me oigas.

So that you can hear me my words become thin sometimes like
the tracks of seagulls on the beach . . . And I look at my so
distant words. More than mine they are yours. They go creep-
ing over my old wound like ivy . . . Before you they inhabited
the solitude that you occupy, and they are accustomed more
than you to my sadness.   Now I want them to say what

I want to say to you so that you can hear me as I want you to hear me.

Again, the repetition of a prosaic formula ("para que tú me oigas") is most effectively used to intrigue the reader, to make him feel like an uneasy witness to an amorous exchange. There is really no exchange, no communication, not in this nor in any of the love poems. The speaker is always alone, the lover is always absent, distant, remote. Thus, the sincerity of the emotion is intensified.

Poem XV is perhaps the best known of the twenty poems of love. It is as familiar to the Hispanic reader of today as was Rubén Darío's "Sonatina" at the turn of the century:

> Me gustas cuando callas porque estás como ausente,
> y me oyes desde lejos, y mi voz no te toca.
> Parece que los ojos se te hubieran volado
> y parece que un beso te cerrara la boca.
>
> Como todas las cosas están llenas de mi alma,
> emerges de las cosas, llena del alma mía.
> Mariposa de sueño, te pareces a mi alma,
> y te pareces a la palabra melancolía.
>
> Me gustas cuando callas y estás como distante.
> Y estás como quejándote, mariposa en arrullo.
> Y me oyes desde lejos, y mi voz no te alcanza:
> Déjame que me calle con el silencio tuyo.
>
> Déjame que te hable también con tu silencio
> claro como una lámpara, simple como un anillo.
> Eres como la noche, callada y constelada.
> Tu silencio es de estrella, tan lejano y sencillo.
>
> Me gustas cuando callas porque estás como ausente.
> Distante y dolorosa como si hubieras muerto.
> Una palabra entonces, una sonrisa bastan.
> Y estoy alegre, alegre de que no sea cierto.

I like you when you are quiet because you are as though absent and you hear me from afar, and my voice doesn't touch you. It seems that your eyes would have flown from you and it seems that a kiss would close your mouth. As all things are filled with my soul, you emerge from things, filled with my soul. Dream butterfly, you are like my soul, and you are like the word melancholy. I like you when you are quiet and you are as though distant. And you are as though complaining, cooing butterfly. And you hear me from afar, and my voice does not reach you: Let me be quiet with your silence. Let me speak to you also with your silence clear as a light, simple as a ring. You are like the night, quiet and stellar. Your silence is of a star, so distant and simple. I like you when you are quiet because you are as though absent. Distant and pitiful as though you had died. One word then, one smile is enough. And I am happy, happy that it is not true.

The form is regular (alexandrines arranged in five symmetric quartets, consonant rhyme in the paired verses) and is a visual and prosodic reminder to the reader that this is a composed poem, a literary construction. In effect, the poem idealizes the sentiment of the book; it glorifies the lover's absence. What is more, it uses simple exhortatory devices (repetition and variation) to stress resonantly the basic themes of incommunicability, distance, and absence ("y me oyes desde lejos, y *mi voz no te toca* . . . y me oyes desde lejos, y *mi voz no te alcanza*"). In recitals this was the composition that Neruda was often requested to read as the most representative of the twenty love poems. Indeed, Poem XV, like the book itself, has meant many different things to as many different people. Neruda himself was puzzled, not by the poem's popularity nor the book's financial success for that matter, but by the real reason for its continued regard. In 1961, commemorating the publication of the millionth copy, he publicly wondered "how this tormented book has, for so many people, been the route to happiness."* For Neruda, the poems were meant to be purgative; for his readers over the years they have come to be inspiring. Well-known and widely imi-

* "Pequeña historia," *Veinte poemas de amor y una canción desesperada* (Buenos Aires, Losada, 1961).

tated, their influence on subsequent love poetry in Spanish has been extraordinary.

When the text first appeared in 1924, poetry was at a crossroads between later Symbolism and the avant-garde, between a renewal of the search for an ever more refined literary expression and the revolutionary notion of the need to update completely the language and the forms of literature: poetry as pure creation versus poetry as pure intuition. Neruda, formed in one tradition and aware of the other (his "Defensa de Vicente Huidobro" is from 1924), chooses a middle ground; he retains the traditional view of the artist as *voyant,* while going on to forge from ordinary experience a new kind of intensity for lyric poetry in Spanish.

Each poem challenges the reader's sensibility in a special way. A new poetic language is created out of an intensely personal system of expression. The verbal interchange in each of the love poems is actually carried out on two levels: the normally unarticulated level of digressive thought, an apparently aimless continuity based on a principle of generative associations; and the ordered, disciplined level of logical discourse. Poem VI, whose content we have previously examined in part, is a conveniently familiar example:

> Te recuerdo como eras en el último otoño.
> Eras la boina gris y el corazón en calma.
> En tus ojos peleaban las llamas del crepúsculo.
> Y las hojas caían en el agua de tu alma.
>
> Apegada a mis brazos como una enredadera,
> las hojas recogían tu voz lenta y en calma.
> Hoguera de estupor en que mi ser ardía.
> Dulce jacinto azul torcido sobre mi alma.
>
> Siento viajar tus ojos y es distante el otoño:
> boina gris, voz de pájaro y corazón de casa
> hacia donde emigraban mis profundos anhelos
> y caían mis besos alegres como brasas.
>
> Cielo desde un navío. Campo desde los cerros.

Tu recuerdo es de luz, de humo, de estanque en calma!
Más allá de tus ojos ardían los crepúsculos.
Hojas secas de otoño giraban en tu alma.

I remember you as you were last Autumn. You were the gray
cap and the heart at peace. In your eyes the flames of the sunset
would do battle. And the leaves would fall in the water of your
soul.   Clinging to my arms like a vine, the leaves would take
in your voice slow and calm. Bonfire of stupor in which my
being blazed. Sweet blue hyacinth twisted over my soul.   I
feel your eyes traveling and Autumn is far away: gray cap, voice
of a bird and heart of home toward which my deepest desires
emigrated and my kisses fell happy like coals.   Sky from a
ship. Fields from the hills. Your remembrance is light, smoke, a
calm well! Beyond your eyes the sunset would blaze. Dry leaves
of Autumn would whirl in your soul.

Four quartets of polyrhythmic alexandrines with a rhyme
scheme that at first glance seems scarcely worthy of a schoolboy.
The repeat rhyme (*calma/alma*) in the second and fourth verses
of each stanza save one (the third) seems at first weak and even
pointless. But then the absence of these words where one has
been conditioned to expect them in the third stanza, and their
substitution with a new pair of terms (*casa/brasa*) in assonance
with the others creates a special kind of resonance and is a
particularly effective use of the basic poetic device of frustrated
expectation. Anticipating *calma/alma* and finding instead *casa/
brasa* calls special attention not only to the missing terms but to
the substitutes as well. Rereading the third stanza, our attention
is drawn to the paradoxical meaning(s) of the concluding simile:
"mis besos alegres como brasas." The fact is that at the level of
logical discourse "alegre" and "brasa" are unrelated terms; this
is an image based not on the classic principle of analogy but on
the avant-garde proposition of the juxtaposition of the dissimi-
lar. We have here several images in one, a poetry that is de-
signedly polysemous. The rhyme pattern encourages the reader
to anticipate "alma" as the term to complete the stanza, an

automatic response which in turn creates another simile, a simile that, if articulated, would more properly pertain to the level of conscious discourse: "mis besos alegres como *mi alma*" (my kisses happy like my soul). The unexpected substitution immediately creates a rich range of associative possibilities both logical and analogical based on a more complex unarticulated composite image: "mis besos alegres como *mi alma y ardientes como* brasas" (my kisses happy like my soul and hot like coals). The same transferral technique is used in the *calma/casa* verses ("corazón en calma . . . corazón de casa"). Neruda thus increases the metaphoric range of his poetry with the simplest of imagery and with an extraordinary economy of means. The entire poem is structured around the idea of loss. Central to its meaning is the familiar seasonal imagery relating to autumn leaves and the inexorable march of time. Simple and familiar terms like "otoño," "crepúsculo," and "hojas secas" create the atmosphere of waning. However, they are used in a novel way. The poem is more than just a momentary evocation of the absent lover; it has a ritual, almost liturgical quality. The lover, elliptically evoked in the first stanza (the famous "boina gris"), in the second and third is litanized through formulaic invocations:

> Hoguera de estupor en que mi ser ardía.
> Dulce jacinto azul torcido sobre mi alma.
> . . . .
> boina gris, voz de pájaro y corazón de casa.

The impossibility of the lovers' ever being reunited is expressed through a masterful adaptation of the basic isosyllabic characteristic of the alexandrine: its ready divisibility into equally balanced hemistiches. Neruda uses this rhythmic division syntactically to present a pair of enigmatic concepts in poised opposition. Again the result is that of transferred meanings: "Cielo desde un navío. Campo desde los cerros." The idea of impossibility suggested by this strange pair of images is thus transferred to the loved one, the remembrance of whom is ephemeral and glacially distant: "Tu recuerdo es de luz, de humo, de estanque en calma." This image from the poem's last stanza resonates with the enigmatic statement of the first: "Y las hojas caían en el agua de tu alma." The implied metaphor, unarticulated here, is *"pozo* de tu alma" (well of your heart). But such a direct enunciation would have marred the delicate tone of the poem. Neruda, by concentrating his expression and by skillfully transferring meanings through an associative process manages to force such a completion of the metaphor to take place in the imagination of the reader. The same technique is employed in yet another statement of the last strophe: "Más allá de tus ojos ardían los crepúsculos," a line which is in resonance with the first strophe's "En tus ojos peleaban las llamas del crepúsculo." At the outset of the poem the sunset potentiated what was once the lover's presence; the last strophe evokes her in an inaccessible beyond, forever distant. Finally, the poem closes with an autonomous image that draws all these diverse ideas together. The changing of the seasons and the waning of love: "Hojas secas de otoño giraban en tu alma." The resultant literary construct affects the reader in a very special way; in this and other texts he must react instinctively. The writing is ostensibly not addressed to him; reading it, he silently and imaginatively recreates its generative process of associations in his mind. In this way the speaker's sentiment is effectively transferred to the reader. For this reason perhaps, these poems, while so disturbing at a first reading, ultimately commit themselves to memory. And it is perhaps for this very same reason that they remain so popular today: the poet creates and the reader recreates an experience, the strongest sense of love and loss, now as then.

But Neruda, having discovered the suggestive power of the autonomous image, would soon put the love poems behind him and embark on a new experiment in creative writing. In an obscure and forgotten note in *Claridad,* June 1924, just after the

publication of *Veinte poemas de amor y una canción deses-
perada* and a few months before the publication of the first
Surrealist manifesto in Paris, Neruda explains a new technique:

> I write and write without being enchained by my thoughts,
> without bothering to free myself from chance associations. . . . I
> let my feelings loose in whatever I write. Disassociated, gro-
> tesque, my writing represents my diverse and discordant depth.
> I build in my words a construct with free matter, and while
> creating I eliminate what has no existence nor any palpable
> hold.*

This was to be the basis for his next major work, *Tentativa del
hombre infinito.*

---

* "Una expresión dispersa," in "Crónica de Sachka," *Claridad* (June
11, 1924), p. 8.

3. The Vanguard Experiment
Tentativa del hombre infinito

> My intention is to get the objective elements out of poetry and to say what I have to say in the most serious way possible.
>
> *1926*

With the publication of the book of love poetry and the favorable and unfavorable reactions that it provoked, Neruda suddenly became a celebrated figure in Santiago. What he said and did was all at once a matter of concern. And much of what he was doing and saying tended to keep him in the public eye. In 1925, for example, he took over the directorship of *Andamios* and converted it from a staid publication of the Federation of Chilean School Teachers into a full-fledged organ of the avant-garde, *Caballo de Bastos*. He was taking his newfound public role as a poet quite seriously, and it is from this period that we have the first of many poses of him strutting about Santiago with a long black cape, presiding over literary banquets, and surrounded by bohemian friends. He was also writing. In 1926 he published three new books, all, incidentally, with Nascimento: *El habitante y su esperanza* (The Inhabitant and His Hope), a novel; *Anillos* (Rings), a volume of experimental prose-pieces written in collaboration with Tomás Lago; and *Tentativa del hombre infinito* (Venture of the Infinite Man), a collection of fifteen new and unusual poems.

Several of the poems had been published separately during the course of 1925. Although they continued for the most part the subject matter of the love poetry, they were written in what seemed to be a much looser and increasingly less structured way. Neruda, like other writers of the avant-garde, had come to forego the use of rhyme, meter, capitalization, and punctuation. Thus, when *Tentativa del hombre infinito* appeared in January 1926, there was much concern over the disintegration of form in his poetry. Predictably, the supporters of Neruda's previous works were the most disillusioned with his latest effort. The Maecenas of *Crepusculario,* Alone, expressed in his newspaper column for Santiago's *La Nación* (January 10, 1926) the fear that the poet had begun to wander along the "route to absurdity"; Raúl Silva Castro, writing in the rival *El Mercurio* (January 31, 1926), was no less distressed:

> If this is poetry, it is naked and anatomic. Skin and bones. The flesh and blood that in the author's other books we had admired so much, fresh and palpitating, are missing here. What we mean to say by this is that the book has no form whatsoever. It is a simple mass of phrases that are not coordinated and among which there are not even any natural or logical separations. There is no punctuation. There are no capitals. One might just as well begin to read from the back as from the front, or even the middle. One would understand the same, that is to say, very little.

Neruda did not have to fight this battle alone though, nor for very long, since the book was well-received outside of Chile. In fact, several poems from *Tentativa* were anthologized that very same year in the *Indice de la nueva poesía americana,* a landmark publication of the avant-garde edited in Buenos Aires by Vicente Huidobro, Alberto Hidalgo, and Jorge Luis Borges. What is more, at about the same time, César Vallejo also reproduced one of the poems (Canto XI) in his Paris-based review of the avant-garde, *Favorables-Paris-Poema.* These poets, then Spanish America's most avant-garde, were able to appreciate what the critics in Chile could not, or did not want to.

Toward the end of 1926, though, the situation in Santiago changed somewhat as Neruda went about explaining his new poetic practice. So persuasive was he at the time that even Raúl Silva Castro did an about-face. After interviewing Neruda for *El Mercurio* in October, he enthusiastically defined the *Tentativa* experiment as something totally new: "The poet has left behind him not only the dead-weight of rhyme and rhythm, but also the unnecessary separation of functions for capital and lower-case letters, relator words, punctuation, etc. Is this poetry? Of course it is. But it is a new kind of poetry."*

What had happened? Neruda's writing had undergone a transformation that, momentarily at least, had thrust him ahead of his critics and interpreters. For this reason he had to go out and explain to them what he was doing. In the same October 1926 interview, Neruda went on to clarify the goals and purposes of his latest work:

> My intention is to get the objective elements out of poetry and to say what I have to say in the most serious way possible. Even proper nouns seem to me false, elements foreign to poetry. In the first canto of *Tentativa* there is a verse that says: "Sólo una estrella inmóvil su fósforo azul" [Just one immobile star its blue phosphorescence]. At first I had written: "Sólo una estrella Sirio su fósforo azul"; but I had to take out of there the noun Sirius, that was too precise, too objective, the unpoetic element of the poem.

Evidently Neruda was striving for a more concentrated literary discourse, one that would convey to the reader the greatest possible degree of subjectivity.

In June 1924, shortly after seeing his love poems into print, he first outlined the reasoning behind what he then termed "Una expresión dispersa" (A Dispersed Expression):

> The vehicles are still circulating outside, a child is crying desperately. I write and write without being enchained by my thoughts, without bothering to free myself from chance

* "Una hora de charla con Pablo Neruda," *El Mercurio*, October 10, 1926.

associations. Simultaneously a thousand admirable things from all around me coincide with the act of creating. They enter by cunning ways into the expression I feel, they secretly produce confused thoughts, they condition, they act upon the end result of meditation itself. Why reject such thoughts? Why even disfigure them? Rather, whatever expression stimulates reality should be included, or be synchonized with the poem. Thought, at every moment, goes beyond the words summoned to express it: it dances; it comes to a stop, and without the need of a trampoline, it ventures to make fateful leaps bringing together the unexpected. To tie up, to discipline into a fixed form this imponderable content, to link it all together with bridges and chains, oh, how criminal! I let my feelings loose in whatever I write. Disassociated, grotesque, my writing represents my diverse and discordant depth. I build in my words a construct with free matter and while creating I eliminate what has no existence nor any palpable hold.*

The writing procedure outlined here coincides with some, but not all, of the postulates of Surrealism. Instead of the "automatisme psychique pur" called for by Breton, Neruda advocates a more controlled kind of literary practice. Automatic writing is not an end in itself, but a useful first step in the elaboration of the poem. Free expression is to be followed by a process of revision, of construction, in which certain elements are eliminated so as to make the text more closely resemble unmediated discourse. Breton wanted to capture the voice of the subconscious; Neruda wanted only to create the style of that voice. To this end, he subjected his *Tentativa* poems to a lengthy process of revision and modification, removing relator words, connectives, and finally even punctuation so as to enhance the run-on associative power of his imagery.

That these changes were not capricious is evident in the periodical literature of the time where early versions of several poems first appeared. In one issue of *Caballo de Bastos* (No. 3, 1925), for example, there are three poems by Neruda. The two

* "Una expresión dispersa," in "Crónica de Sachka."

unpunctuated items, "Canto de las ansiedades" (Song of Anxieties) and "Poesía escrita de noche" (Poetry Written at Night), would later appear in *Tentativa del hombre infinito* (Cantos XI, XIII), while the third, "Serenata" (Serenade), employing punctuation and a traditional use of typography, would eventually form part of *Residencia en la tierra*. Neruda was obviously aware of the different effects to be obtained with and without punctuation.

Most readers in 1926 reacted, quite naturally, to what *Tentativa* did not have. The book's so-called "formlessness" was then most disturbing; even the pages were unnumbered. Today we can view the same book from a postvanguard perspective and see it for what it actually does contain: fifteen separate compositions of unique and varied strophic patterns. In the love poems Neruda had experimented with a new kind of lyric discourse; in *Tentativa del hombre infinito* he gives this discourse a new form. The result is a highly cohesive work.

If we return to the original text we can see that the series of cantos was arranged according to a definite plan whose unity—dissembled in subsequent printings—was rather prominently stressed in 1926 through a prefatory declaration immediately following the title page: "Poema de Pablo Neruda" (A Poem by Pablo Neruda). This announced poematic unity is more than confirmed in the system of textual correlations which artfully bring the cantos together in a singularly coherent whole. The sequential organization is particularly evident: moving from dusk ("a la siga de la noche"—in pursuit of the night [Canto III] to dawn ("a la siga del alba"—in pursuit of dawn [Canto XIII]), the poem is patterned around the theme of the imaginary voyage ("embarcado en ese viaje nocturno"—embarked on this nocturnal voyage [Canto XIII]) as a personal quest for the absolute.

The disciplined organization of each of the separate cantos is visually apparent from the outset. In the first, for example, the perfect symmetry of the strophic arrangement gives a sense of balance to the disquiet of the nocturnal scene:

hogueras pálidas revolviéndose al borde de las noches
corren humos difuntos polvaredas invisibles

fraguas negras durmiendo detrás de los cerros anochecidos
la tristeza del hombre tirada entre los brazos del sueño

ciudad desde los cerros en la noche los segadores duermen
debatida a las últimas hogueras
pero estás allí pegada a tu horizonte
como una lancha al muelle lista para zarpar lo creo
antes del alba

árbol de estertor candelabro de llamas viejas
distante incendio mi corazón está triste

sólo una estrella inmóvil su fósforo azul
los movimientos de la noche aturden hacia el cielo

(Canto I)

pallid fires turning about at the edge of the nights dead smoke invisible dust clouds race on   black forges sleeping behind darkened hills the sadness of man tossed in the arms of sleep   city from the hills at night the reapers sleep debated at the last fires but you are there pegged to your horizon like a ship at the dock ready to sail I believe at dawn   tree of creaks candelabra of old flames distant fire my heart is sad   only one star immobile its blue phosphorescence the movements of the night agitate toward the sky.

Here the suppression of punctuation has the obvious effect of making the reader more sensitive to other basic modulating devices such as strophic unity and the syntactic order of the discontinuous discourse. Thus, the imagery may readily be seen to be organized around the single, almost elemental simile of the central strophe comparing the city lights on the horizon to those of a ship readying to sail at dawn ("ciudad desde los cerros . . . como una lancha al muelle"). The opening and closing strophes, devoid of subjective referents, serve as a kind of objective frame to the tristesse expressed in the intermediate couplets which, in turn, envelop the lyric content at the core of the canto. The lack of punctuation is no mere vanguardist caprice, but a sophisticated literary device largely responsible for the poem's run-on quality, its curious sense of suspension amidst seemingly perpetual motion. Some idea of the calculated effectiveness of the artifice can be gleaned from the opening couplets where the rush of the unpunctuated lines is fixed in each strophe by parallel gerundial constructions that attribute a certain atemporal quality to the verbal process and give a kind of substantive permanence to the imagery of flux. A flux, moreover, whose enduring character is controlled throughout the rest of the canto by the consistent use of the present tense in the conjugated verbs, a maneuver which tends even further to freeze the motion, to lock it into perpetuity. The net result rather resembles a movie still, or, perhaps more precisely, a series of stills. Each strophe presents an arrested image of an action.

Extending the analogy with film offers some insight into the process of the canto's movement. At the risk of oversimplification, a "zoom" effect seems to have been achieved in the succession of images from strophe to strophe. Holding the point of view constant while the angle of vision is changed permits the first couplet's mysterious fulgor of fire to come into view sequentially as the flickering of the city lights, a moored ship, a candelabra, stars, and finally a single star, the brightest in the firmament (Sirius, in an earlier version). The vision is completed through a sequence of images whose associative element—light at night—brings together the counterpoised descriptions of the earth and the sky which frame the composition.

The suppression of punctuation is an artistic aid to the extent that it permits a loosening of the discourse, thus making possible in the first canto the special kind of elliptic continuity that results in the composite, cosmic vision of the nocturnal void. In this way Neruda succeeds in presenting a new version of an old theme: the nocturne; poetized not in the traditional fashion of mysterious divagation, but from the vanguard position of marvelous reality, a prelude to the book's principal theme—the "viaje nocturno," the nocturnal voyage.

Tentativa del hombre infinito was an ambitious undertaking for Neruda at the time. Describing an imaginary sleepwalk through space and time, he arranged the book's fifteen separate cantos in an interrelated series making up the classic pattern of a quest. If we look at the second canto we can appreciate how it was made to resonate with the first through a kind of verbal parallelism:

> *ciudad desde los cerros* entre la noche de hojas
> mancha amarilla su rostro abre la sombra
> mientras *tendido sobre el pasto* deletreo
> ahí pasan ardiendo sólo yo vivo
>
> *tendido sobre el pasto mi corazón está triste*
> la luna azul araña trepa inunda
>
> emisario ibas alegre en la tarde que caía
> el crepúsculo rodaba apagando flores
>
> *tendido sobre el pasto* hecho de tréboles negros
> y tambalea sólo su pasión delirante
>
> recoge una mariposa húmeda como un collar
> anúdame tu cinturón de estrellas esforzadas
>
> (Canto II, emphasis mine)

city from the hills in the night of leaves yellow stain your face opens the shadow while spread out on the grass I am spelling out there they pass along blazing only I am alive   spread out on the grass my heart is sad the blue moon scratches creeps inundates   emissary you were going along happy in the afternoon that was falling the twilight rolled on putting out flowers   spread out on the grass made of black clovers and only its delirious passion totters   grab a butterfly humid as a necklace fasten me with your cinch of striving stars.

The same syntagmas ("ciudad desde los cerros," "mi corazón está triste") around which the basic imagery of the book's opening verses had been organized are here strategically repeated for an effect which is both unifying and episodic; in resonance with the nocturnal metaphor of the first canto, they serve now to make the solitary figure of the speaker stand out as he is imagistically linked to the previous description of the night. Syntagmatic repetition, strophic unity, even the prosaic positioning of the temporal adverb ("mientras," while) all combine to highlight the narrator's role as protagonist in the creative present of the poem: "ciudad desde los cerros . . . mientras tendido sobre el pasto deletreo . . . mi corazón está triste." The result is a composite vision of the somnambular lyric poet as narrator-protagonist alone in the nocturnal void.

The strophic distribution of the second canto is a unique controlling device no less significant than that of the first: descriptive symmetry cedes to an accumulative sequence of verbal actions in which the narrative tense is made to shift from the present to the past and back again to the present in a staccato delivery of lyric sensations. Through a succession of discrete strophic visions, verbs of aimless striving ("trepar," "rodar," "tambalear") accumulate in intensity while a new syntagma of position ("tendido sobre el pasto") emerges to function as an imagistic anchor for the structured view of the poet as narrator, participant, and witness of the nocturnal quest. The second canto thus effectively builds upon the first: moving in a similar fashion from the glow of the city lights to the flickering of the stars, the sudden identification of the speaker as protagonist and the subsequent layering of short strophes combine to increase the tempo of the yearning for cosmic communion so urgently voiced—"tendido sobre el pasto"—in the canto's closing verse: "anúdame tu cinturón de estrellas esforzadas."

Neruda's artistic approach to the personal, experiential dimension of the poem is now quite different, although as in the love poetry, his frustrated affair with Albertina is still the source of inspiration. We may recall that in one of the letters of the period, he had written: "Spread out on the grass, in the evenings, I dream of your gray cap, of your eyes that I love, of you. I go out every night at around five, to wander around the deserted streets, to wander through the countryside."* The dif-

* *Cartas de amor de Pablo Neruda*, p. 202.

ference between the two books, between the two kinds of discourse in *Tentativa* and the love poetry, is a difference of purpose. The poems of love were entreaties to an absent lover; the cantos purport to be the somnambulistic ramblings of a preconscious state of mind. Hence, the importance of a certain amount of reader confusion and the variety of devices employed to maintain an air of uncertainty and vagueness.

The entire book is a vanguard experiment in different styles and techniques. For example, in the third canto, when the "nocturnal voyage" actually gets under way, the measured strophic divisions of the earlier compositions are abandoned in favor of a single unit of nineteen uninterrupted lines simulating the headlong rush into the vortex of the night. In this manner the poetic voice in the canto of departure achieves a subtle distancing effect, building up to the ecstasy of a participant, before shifting over to the lyric "you," and finally fading out to that of an impersonal observer:

> oh matorrales crespos adonde el sueño avanza trenes
> oh montón de tierra entusiasta donde de pie sollozo
> vértebras de la noche agua tan lejos viento intranquilo rompes
> también estrellas crucificadas detrás de la montaña
> alza su empuje un ala pasa un vuelo oh noche sin llaves
> oh noche mía en mi hora en mi hora furiosa y doliente
> eso me levantaba como la ola al alga
> acoge mi corazón desventurado
> cuando rodeas los animales del sueño
> crúzalo con tus vastas correas de silencio
> está a tus pies esperando una partida
> porque lo pones cara a cara a ti misma noche de hélices negras
> y que toda fuerza en él sea fecunda
> atada al cielo con estrellas de lluvia
> procrea tú amárrate a esa proa minerales azules
> *embarcado en ese viaje nocturno*
> *un hombre de veinte años sujeta una rienda frenética*
> *es que él quería ir a la siga de la noche*
> *entre sus manos ávidas el viento sobresalta*
>
> (Canto III, emphasis mine)

oh crisp-leaved thickets toward which sleep advances trains /
oh mound of enthusiastic earth where standing up I sob /
vertebrates of night water so distant restless wind you break /
also crucified stars behind the mountain / raise up its thrust a
wing passes a flight oh night without keys / oh night of mine
in my hour in my furious and pained hour / that lifted me up
like algae on the wave / sieze my unfortunate heart / when
you surround the animals of sleep / crisscross it with your vast
straps of silence / it is at your feet awaiting a departure / be-
cause you put it face to face to yourself night of black propel-
lers / and may all force in it be fecund / tide to the sky with
stars of rain / procreate hitch yourself up to that prow blue
minerals / embarked in this nocturnal voyage / a man of
twenty holds on to a frantic rein / it is that he wanted to go
off in pursuit of the night / between his hands the wind leaps
forth.

Whereas the first person is used to express the physical sensation
of being immersed in the night—"eso me levantaba como la ola
al alga" (that lifted me up like algae on the wave)—the third
person is relied upon to achieve a certain narrative distance, to
objectify the cosmic voyage, even prosaically to explain the
motivation for embarking—"es que él quería ir a la siga de la
noche" (it is that he wanted to go off in pursuit of the night).

Tentativa del hombre infinito belongs to the tradition of the
modern voyage poem. While it undoubtedly has its origin in
certain earlier efforts (Rimbaud, "Le Bateau ivre"; Baudelaire,
"Le Voyage"), in the context of the Hispanic avant-garde it
turns out to be seminal to the development of the book-length
metaphysical poem (Alberti, *Sobre los ángeles;* Huidobro,
Altazor; Gorostiza, *Muerte sin fin*): a poetic venture based on
the illuminating concept of the mythic quest. To this end, the
first three cantos fall into an epic pattern of departure: the
scene is set, the call is received, the quest is undertaken. In the
next three (IV-VI), after the imaginary voyage begins, another
pattern emerges as the hero is subjected to a series of trials,
the rites of passage.

As the adventure continues to unfold, the camera-eye objectivity of the earlier narrative style is replaced with a new loquaciousness communicating a sense of participatory awe and wonder; the protagonist, loosed of terrestrial bonds, experiences the nocturnal phenomena from a changed and changing perspective. Certain imagistic constants drawn from the introductory cantos are used to create an effect of narrative continuity. Not surprisingly, Sirius, the "estrella inmóvil" that closed the hermetic metaphor of the first canto, reappears transmogrified at the opening of the fourth: "estrella retardada entre la noche gruesa" (star bogged down in the thick night). Starry imagery remains central to the other compositions as well. In the sixth canto the vast void of night is figuratively conquered, hyperbolically envisioned as an inverted well: "los ojos caían en ese pozo inverso / hacia donde ascendía la soledad de todo" (the eyes fell down into that inverted well toward which the solitude of everything was ascending). Accordingly, the tone of the narrative voice changes, and the somnambulic poet finally begins to speak out with a pronounced assurance.

At the outset, syntagmatic repetition was used to fix the narrative situation of the imaginary voyage ("tendido sobre el pasto deletreo" [Canto II]); now ellipsis is used for an almost breathless effect, running together imagery of joy and loquacity as the speaker whirls on into the center of the night:

> no sé hacer el canto de los días
> sin querer suelto el canto la alabanza de las noches
> pasó el viento latigándome la espalda alegre saliendo de su
>   huevo
> descienden las estrellas a beber al océano
>
> (Canto VI)

I don't know how to make a daytime canto / without wanting to I let loose the canto the praise of night / the wind passed by whipping my back happy coming out of its egg / the stars descend to drink in the ocean.

Midway through the book, in Cantos VII-IX, there is a kind of climax, an encounter with the night itself that is poetized in a lyric style not unlike that of *Veinte poemas de amor*. In Canto VII physical union realized through the sexual act becomes a metaphor for ultimate oneness: "torciendo hacia ese lado o más allá continúas siendo mía . . . en otra parte lejos existen tú y yo parecidos a nosotros" (turning toward that side or farther away you continue being mine . . . in another place far away you and I exist something like ourselves). And in the ninth canto the body of woman is directly metaphorized as the vehicle of ecstasy, the "navío blanco" (white ship) of the imaginary voyage:

> ah para qué alargaron la tierra
> del lado en que te miro y no estás niña mía
> entre sombra y sombra destino de naufragio
> nada tengo oh soledad
> sin embargo eres la luz distante que ilumina las frutas
> y moriremos juntos
> pensar que estás ahí navío blanco listo para partir
> y que tenemos juntas las manos en la proa navío siempre en
>   viaje

> ah why did they stretch out the earth / on the side from which I am looking at you and you are not there my little girl / between shadow and shadow destiny of shipwreck / I have nothing oh solitude / nevertheless you are the distant light that illuminates the fruit / and we shall die together / to think that you are there white ship ready to depart / and that we have our hands joined at the prow ship always in motion.

After the cosmic union is realized the speaker's references to himself become more explicit. In the latter portion of the poem —less cinematically descriptive and more impressionistically memory-oriented—movement between the narrative present and the remembered past is generally compressed in the same strophe, a device that effectively serves to contemporize the flashbacks:

ésta es mi casa
aún la perfuman los bosques
desde donde la acarreaban
allí tricé mi corazón como el espejo para andar a través de mi
   mismo

. . . .

yo no cuento yo digo en palabras desgraciadas
aún los andamios dividen el crepúsculo
y detrás de los vidrios la luz del petróleo
era para mirar hacia el cielo

                           (Canto X)

this is my house / even now the forests perfume it / from
where it was carted in / there I shattered my heart like a mirror
in order to walk through myself . . . I don't tell stories I say
it outright in words without grace / even now the scaffolding
divides the twilight / and behind the windows the petroleum
lamp / was for looking up at the sky.

The clipped assertive narration is characteristic of the later
cantos (X-XII) and stands in sharp contrast with the lyricism of
the central portion of the poem. Hyperbole is now reversed and
used to augment the role of the narrator rather than merely to
reduce that of the universe. In Canto X's verses the unfinished
house of the poet's birth, without walls or roof, is aggrandized;
the scaffolding is viewed as superimposed on the sunset, while
the artificial light of the house-lamp is seen to illumine the sky.
This is the kind of creative liberty with language made possible
by the experimental attitude of the avant-garde. But *Tentativa
del hombre infinito* is primarily a poematic quest for the abso-
lute and only secondarily an experiment with new writing
techniques; Neruda, mindful of his narrative plan, keeps his
hero moving on toward a kind of atonement with the past. At
one point though, the narrator becomes engaged, *Residencia*-
like, in a meditative search for self:

admitiendo el cielo profundamente mirando el cielo estoy
   pensando

con inseguridad sentado en ese borde
oh cielo tejido con aguas y papeles
comencé a hablarme en voz baja decidido a no salir
arrastrado por la respiración de mis raíces
inmóvil navío ávido de esas leguas azules

(Canto XI)

letting the sky in profoundly looking at the sky I am thinking /
with insecurity seated on the edge / oh sky woven with water
and papers / I began to speak to myself in a low voice decided
not to come out / dragged along by the respiration of my
roots / immobile ship avid for those blue leagues.

In the concluding portion of the book Neruda utilizes with
particular effectiveness the avant-garde technique of juxtapo-
sition. The narrator, denied his camera-eye objectivity and
stripped of his neoromantic role as anxious participant of the
cosmic flux, emerges most concretely toward the end in the
assigned role of "hombre infinito" (infinite man). In Canto XIII,
as the nocturnal adventure draws to a close—"el alba se divisa"
(dawn is visible)—time and space are stretched out and treated
materially in a unique imagistic recital of the hero's return:

el mes de junio se extendió de repente en el tiempo con seriedad
   y exactitud
como un caballo y en el relámpago crucé la orilla
ay el crujir del aire pacífico era muy grande

(Canto XIV)

the month of June suddenly extended itself in time with
seriousness and exactitude / like a horse and on a lightning
bolt I crossed over the edge / ay the creaking of the peaceful
air was very great.

The fifteenth canto functions as a kind of epilogue and,
through the reuse of certain expressions drawn from the earlier
cantos (for example, "mi corazón está cansado"), ties together
the narrative plan of the work: "estoy de pie en la luz como el

medio día en la tierra / quiero contarlo todo con ternura" (I am standing up in the light like midday on the earth / I want to tell it all with tenderness). Anticipating yet another nightfall, the poem's closure implies a certain cyclical continuity:

> espérame donde voy ah el atardecer
> la comida las barcarolas de océano oh espérame
> adelantándote como ˙un grito atrasándote como una huella oh
>   espérate
> sentado en esa última sombra o todavía después
> todavía
>
> (Canto XV)

> wait for me where I am going ah the evening comes / the dinner the ocean boats oh wait for me / getting ahead of you like a shout getting behind you like a footstep oh wait up / seated on this last shadow or still later / still.

At the end, as at the beginning, the gerundial run-on constructions and the accumulative repetition of temporal adverbs combine effectively to lock the poematic quest in a timeless present.

This is a major work. It brought the interior monologue into Neruda's poetry without the Surrealist dependence on automatic writing. Moreover, this book, for its innovative use of language and its highly charged lyric content, constitutes the link between two extraordinary masterpieces: *Veinte poemas de amor* and *Residencia en la tierra*. Yet, for all its perfection, it never gained the readership Neruda wanted it to have. Accepted only by the literary avant-garde when it first appeared, it was quickly passed over and was all but forgotten until quite recently. Over the years Neruda, continuing his campaign of 1926, kept on insisting that critics go back and read this work to find the origins of his disciplined approach to poetry. In 1964, for example, we find him stressing the seminal importance of the *Tentativa* experiment:

Tentativa del hombre infinito is a book that did not achieve what I wanted it to, it was not successful for a variety of reasons in which even day to day circumstances intervened. Nevertheless, even with its smallness and its minimal expression, it assured more than any other work of mine, the path I was to follow. I have always looked upon *Tentativa del hombre infinito* as one of the real nuclei of my poetry, because working on those poems, in those now distant years, I was acquiring a consciousness that I didn't have before, and if my expressions, their clarity or mystery, are anywhere measured, it is in this little book.*

Neruda was right of course. And, in the context of his own evolution, it seems clear that around 1925 he began to forsake the refined prosodic system of Hispanic poetry; he then managed to creatively combine the liberties of the literary avant-garde with such elemental and seemingly artless devices as the parallelism of key syntactic units, the modulation of the poetic line, the organizational power of the strophe, and the disciplined use of the quest theme in order to structure the fifteen cantos of his *Tentativa del hombre infinito* in the meaningful trajectory of a voyage through space and time in search of the absolute. To be sure, the quest for ultimate oneness was one of the constants in the later Modernist literature of Spain and Spanish America, and it was essentially from this aesthetic perspective that Neruda himself had earlier dealt with the theme in the final poem ("La canción desesperada") of his *Veinte poemas de amor y una canción desesperada*. However, only after abandoning the hollow shell of rhyme and meter and freeing his expression from the logical concatenation of continuous discourse was Neruda able to attain the unusual inner cohesion and high degree of poetic tension that stylistically link his vanguard experiment of 1926 to the expressive system of the *Residencia* cycle.

* "Algunas reflexiones improvisadas sobre mis trabajos," *Mapocho*, 2:180–181 (1964).

4. Hermeticism
The Residencia Cycle

The world has changed, and my poetry with it.

1939

The success of the love poems in 1924 fixed the pen name of Pablo Neruda and established its user as an important new figure in Chilean literature. Subsequent experiments with vanguard techniques in *Tentativa del hombre infinito* carried the young poet out of a provincial orbit and assured him of a more than local fame. However, it was only after the publication of *Residencia en la tierra* in 1933 that Neruda was widely hailed internationally not simply as another good poet but as the major new poet of the Spanish language. When he arrived in Madrid as Consul in 1935 the most prominent younger writers of Spain such as Federico García Lorca, Jorge Guillén, and Rafael Alberti banded together to manifest publicly their admiration for his work, a contribution that, in their words, "constitutes without dispute one of the most authentic realities of poetry in the Spanish language today."*

---

* Other signatories to the *Homenaje a Pablo Neruda de los poetas españoles* (Madrid, Plutarco, 1935), which contained a special edition of his "Tres cantos materiales," three poems from *Residencia en la tierra,* were: Vicente Aleixandre, Manuel Altolaguirre, Luis Cernuda, Gerardo Diego, León Felipe, Pedro Salinas, Miguel Hernández, José A. Muñoz Rojas, Leopoldo and Juan Panero, Luis Rosales, Arturo Serrano Plaja, and Luis Felipe Vivanco.

Why and how did this poetry suddenly generate such widespread admiration? Parnassus is not often so quickly scaled. In Neruda's case a combination of circumstances in which strategy and chance played equal roles helped the poets of his generation to perceive what it took the critics much longer to realize: *Residencia en la tierra* furnished a new and modern diction to poetry in Spanish. This system of expression, so appropriate to the existential concerns of modern Hispanic authors, was so inextricably linked to the person of Neruda, that others who wrote in the same vein in Spain and Spanish America were quickly, perhaps too quickly, dubbed "nerudianos" and the hermetic modality they practiced "Nerudism." Although the Chilean's poetry was to change with time, the term would remain to categorize hauntingly what in other literatures, Italian, for example, has somewhat more objectively been described as hermeticism. For this reason, in a retrospective view of Neruda's work of this period fact must be separated from fancy, the purely literary from the merely legendary, in order to arrive at an accurate appreciation of what is truly unique in the literature of the so-called *Residencia* cycle.

The cycle has an interesting history. After the local impact of *Veinte poemas de amor y una canción desesperada* and the later international resonance of *Tentativa del hombre infinito*, Neruda was recognized as a man of letters, both within and without Chile. He then sought and obtained a post in his country's diplomatic corps—not an unusual occupation for a successful poet in South America. Assigned as Consul to Rangoon in 1927, he began to send back for publication in the Chilean press travel notes, impressions, and poems recording his new experiences in the Far East. The disciplined concentration of this patently occasional literature reveals a shift away from the exuberant lyricism of his earlier work. Neruda stressed the literary significance of this change in letters to his friends. As early as 1928, he wrote to the Chilean novelist José

Santos González Vera about a new book of poems to be called
Residencia en la tierra:

> My latest work has achieved a great perfection (or imperfec-
> tion). That is to say, I have passed a literary limit that I
> never believed myself capable of surpassing, and to tell the
> truth, the results surprise me and console me. My new book
> shall be called *Residencia en la tierra* and it will contain forty
> poems in verse that I want to publish in Spain.*

Various complications, not the least of which was Neruda's
persistent ambition to publish in Spain, stalled the appearance
of this portentous work until 1933. And even then it was pub-
lished not in Spain but in Chile, and in a limited edition. Its
carefully elaborated poems numbered thirty-three and com-
prised compositions written between 1925 and 1931. In 1935,
having finally found a suitable publisher in Spain, Neruda
reedited this first volume of *Residencia en la tierra* and added
a second, a continuation, with twenty-three more poems. The
strategy was correct, for these two volumes, published in Ma-
drid on the eve of the Spanish Civil War, would secure his
fame. With the triumph of the combined edition of *Residencia
en la tierra,* Neruda's creative energies were freed to work on a
third volume of poetry. At this point, during the war years,
he began to emerge as a socially committed poet. In 1947 he
collected his writing for the period 1935–1945 under the title
Tercera residencia. These three volumes, containing all Ne-
ruda's poetry from a twenty-year period (1925–1945) predate
Canto general (1950), the lengthy epic on man's struggle for
justice in the New World, and thus constitute what has come
to be called the *Residencia* cycle.

The closed time interval, spanning two decades, and the
sequential title combine to imply a stylistic and thematic con-
tinuity that is not always borne out by the poetry itself. Re-

* Letter of August 6, 1928, reproduced in Hernán Loyola, *Ser y morir
en Pablo Neruda* (Santiago, Editora Santiago, 1967), pp. 84–85.

reading these three volumes today, it is apparent that the first is introspective and existential, while the second is more discursive and less anguished. The third, *Tercera residencia,* is decidedly political. Only through a comparative book-by-book examination of the elements of change and continuity in each of these three works can we hope to arrive at an accurate determination of the qualities, both specific and general, of the poetry somewhat loosely considered to make up the *Residencia* cycle.

Residencia en la tierra I (1925–1931)

I have described how Neruda, on his return to Chile from the Far East in 1932, arranged to publish his poetry with Nascimento in a deluxe limited edition. This text, of a grand format (27 x 36 cm.), was hailed as a major work in early 1933 by those fortunate enough to obtain a copy. Time has confirmed the original judgment of the book's importance, although for somewhat different aesthetic reasons. What was unique then is less so today. There was much polite discussion at that time concerning certain unusual qualities of this enigmatic text, notably its prosaic rhetoric and its profound pessimism. Postwar enchantment with existentialism has legitimated a pessimistic attitude in literature, and prosaism has come to be accepted as a norm of modern poetry. Thus, the reader of today is not likely to be stunned by the opening poem of *Residencia en la tierra,* somewhat puzzlingly titled "Galope muerto" (Death Gallop or Gallop toward Death; not Dead Gallop as it is sometimes translated):

> Como cenizas, como mares poblándose,
> en la sumergida lentitud, en lo informe,
> o como se oyen desde el alto de los caminos
> cruzar las campanadas en cruz,
> teniendo ese sonido ya aparte del metal,
> confuso, pesando, haciéndose polvo
> en el mismo molino de las formas demasiado lejos,

o recordadas o no vistas,
y el perfume de las ciruelas que rodando a tierra
se pudren en el tiempo, infinitamente verdes.

Aquello todo tan rápido, tan viviente,
inmóvil sin embargo, como la polea loca en sí misma,
esas ruedas de los motores, en fin.
Existiendo como las puntadas secas en las costuras del árbol,
callado, por alrededor, de tal modo,
mezclando todos los limbos sus colas.
Es que de dónde, en qué orilla?
El rodeo constante incierto, tan mudo,
como las lilas alrededor del convento,
o la llegada de la muerte a la lengua del buey
que cae a tumbos, guardabajo, y cuyos cuernos quieren sonar.

Por eso, en lo inmóvil, deteniéndose, percibir,
entonces, como aleteo inmenso, encima,
como abejas muertas, o números,
ay lo que mi corazón pálido no puede abarcar,
en multitudes, en lágrimas saliendo apenas,
y esfuerzos humanos, tormentas,
acciones negras descubiertas de repente
como hielos, desorden vasto,
oceánico, para mí que entro cantando,
como con una espada entre indefensos.

Ahora bien, de qué está hecho ese surgir de palomas
que hay entre la noche y el tiempo, como una barranca húmeda?
Ese sonido ya tan largo
que cae listando de piedras los caminos,
más bien, cuando sólo una hora
crece de improviso, extendiéndose sin tregua.

Adentro del anillo del verano
una vez los grandes zapallos escuchan,
estirando sus plantas conmovedoras,
de eso, de lo que solicitándose mucho,
de lo lleno, oscuros de pesadas gotas.

Like ashes, like seas peopling themselves, in the submerged
slowness, in the unformed, or as heard from the height of the

roads the crisscrossing of tolling bells, having that sound already
separated from the metal, confused, weighted down, becoming
dust in the same mill of forms too far away, or remembered
or not seen, and the perfume of plums that rolling to the ground
rot in time, infinitely green.   All that so rapid, so alive, im-
mobile nevertheless, like a loose pulley, those wheels of motors,
in short. Existing like dry stitches on the bark of trees, silent,
all around, in such a way, entwining the edges of all limbos.
From where is it, by what way, on what shore? The constant
rotation, uncertain, so mute, like the lilacs around the convent
or the arrival of death on the tongue of an ox that falls tum-
bling, chest down, and whose horns want to bellow.   For that
reason, in the unmoveable, stopping to perceive, then, like an
immense flutter, above, like dead bees, or numbers, alas, what
my pale heart can not embrace, in multitudes, in tears hardly
shed, and human efforts, storms, black actions discovered sud-
denly like ice, vast disorder, oceanic, for me who enters singing
as though with a sword among the defenseless.   Now then,
of what is made this surging of doves what is between the night
and time, like a wet ravine? That sound already so long that
it falls striping the roads with stones, rather, when only an hour
grows unexpectedly, extending itself relentlessly.   Within the
ring of summer one time enormous pumpkins are listening,
stretching out their emotive roots, of this, of what is being so
much solicited, full, dark with heavy drops.

Readers conditioned to the subtle logic of symbolist verse
were once concerned with the odd way each of the poem's first
four strophes begins. Relative adverbs and demonstrative pro-
nouns are used to give an aura of authoritative certainty to
what is otherwise unclear. The obscurity is intentional, as is
the rhetorical prosaism which draws attention to it. The first
strophe, for example, of some ten lines, is organized as a single
phrase, an incomplete phrase. The accumulative repetition of
"como," the familiar comparative term of most similes in
Spanish, reminds the reader that the comparison is incomplete.
He is linguistically conditioned to expect a joining of images
which in fact never takes place; he is never informed of just

what is being compared with what. This expectation, frustrated in the opening strophe, is basic to the entire poem.

The second strophe begins with a demonstrative construction ("Aquello todo," All that), which too implies a logical continuity that is not forthcoming; and the adverbial locutions ("Por eso," For that reason, "Ahora bien," Now then), which give false starts to the third and fourth strophes, serve a similar purpose. The poem is not based on external correspondences; it relates inward, upon itself. Not a composition about something definite or even an autonomous invention as in the best tradition of the avant-garde, it is instead a poetization of undefined experience. The speaker of the poem seems to feel the world and register his impression of it without need of further explanation. Meaning is not imposed. The result is a poetry not of immediate insight but of gradual discernment, a growing awareness that is systematically transferred to the text of the poem, even in violation of normal Spanish syntax as though to demonstrate its pre-logical quality. This apparently is the purpose of the many verbs in the participial form, functioning as gerunds ("como mares poblándose . . . haciéndose polvo . . . rodando a tierra"—like seas peopling themselves . . . becoming dust . . . rolling to the ground). The idea conveyed is that of an eternal process of becoming, the participial expression effectively eternalizing the described action. Action occurs without beginning or end, in a seemingly eternal process, whose meaning is rhetorically questioned by the poem's speaker in the second strophe:

> Es que de dónde, por dónde, en qué orilla?
> El rodeo constante incierto, tan mudo.

Similar queries, always without answers, are dispersed throughout the poem. The effect is disquieting. All this activity, this rush toward nothingness, seems so pointless, so utterly meaningless. Yet the poem concludes on this affirmative note:

Adentro del anillo del verano
una vez los grandes zapallos escuchan,
estirando sus plantas conmovedoras,
de eso, de lo que solicitándose mucho,
de lo lleno, oscuros de pesadas gotas.

The plants grow; life goes on. But the poet conveys only this. Writers of a happier epoch used plants and flowers as symbols for nature's ceaseless process of renewal. Such a felicitous "discovery" would often prompt philosophic conclusions concerning the continuity of life, the generations of man, the progress of the universe. Neruda's posture is not so feigned. He does not explain anything more, for in truth he cannot. But he too goes on, in spite of the seeming indifference of the universe and the lack of universal meaning. This is the theme of the first *Residencia en la tierra*: the perpetual disintegration of life, the headlong rush toward death so succinctly expressed in the title of "Galope muerto."

Neruda is a poet and not a philosopher, and it is not my intention to stress inordinately the possible metaphysical bases of his literature. Especially when in one of this volume's prose poems, "El deshabitado" (The Uninhabited), recreating a standard situation of literary impressionism, the isolating density of a fog, the speaker adamantly refuses to philosophize, to speculate on the meaning of what is beyond the immediately discernible:

De modo que el ser se sentía aislado, sometido a esa extraña substancia, rodeado de un cielo próximo, con el mástil quebrado frente a un litoral blanquecino, abandonado de lo sólido, frente a un transcurso impenetrable y en una casa de niebla. Condenación y horror! De haber estado herido y abandonado, o haber escogido las arañas, el luto y la sotana. De haberse emboscado, fuertemente ahito de este mundo, y de haber conversado esfinges y oros y fatídicos destinos. De haber amarrado la ceniza al traje cotidiano, y haber besado el origen terrestre con su sabor a olvido. Pero no. No.

So that the individual felt himself isolated, given up to this strange substance, surrounded by a closed sky, with the mast broken before a pallid shore, abandoned by the solid element, faced by an impenetrable distance and in a house of fog. Condemnation and horror! To have been wounded and abandoned, or to have chosen the spiders, mourning and the cassock. To have hidden oneself, strongly fed up with this world, and to have conversed of sphinxes, and gold and fateful destinies. To have grasped the ashes of quotidian clothes, and to have kissed the terrestrial origin with its taste of oblivion. But no. No.

As the prose poem concludes, Neruda permits only a restatement of the same experience in a somewhat more objectively concentrated style. He poetizes the materiality of solitude, and this alone:

Materias frías de la lluvia que caen sombríamente, pesares sin resurrección, olvido. En mi alcoba sin retratos, en mi traje sin luz, cuánta cabida eternamente permanece, y el lento rayo recto del día cómo se condensa hasta llegar a ser una sola gota oscura.

Cold materials of the rain that somberly fall, sorrows without resurrection, oblivion. In my bedroom without portraits, in my suit without lights, how much space remains eternally, and the slow straight beam of day how it is condensed until becoming one single dark drop.

There is an implied metaphysical attitude here, recognizable today as existential: man adrift in an indifferent world. But if this is so, and if the poet is sincere, why does he write? What is the function of poetry in such a bleak and barren universe? The answer to this question is to be found in Neruda's essentially neoromantic concept of the poet as *vates,* as the inspired voice of the voiceless. This attitude, which informed *Crepusculario,* was explicitly advanced in Neruda's own exegesis of *Veinte poemas de amor y una canción desesperada*: "freely, incontainably, my poems set themselves loose from me." The artist as a volcano of creative energy: most nineteenth- and early-twentieth-century poetics subscribe to this view and differ only in their interpretation of the ways in which this efflux might best be disciplined and channeled into art. *Residencia en la tierra* is part of this tradition, though, in it Neruda seems less concerned with theory and more with practice. The work is unique in that it does not attempt to justify itself internally. There is little internal reference to how or even why it was written. The poems, covering a diverse range of topics from monsoons to marriage, are arranged more or less chronologically.

The first and longest section, containing twenty poems, includes the earliest and most hermetic compositions—those written in Chile during a period of intense avant-garde experimentation (1925–1927) as well as those written in the stylized literary posture of the isolating density of the Far East experience (1927–1929). The third and fourth sections taken together contain only seven poems, all written after 1929, and are by far the most discursive, at times even anecdotal. The most curious section in this book is the second, which contains only prose. In an age of free verse, what is the function of a poem in prose? Why insert prose in a collection of verse? "El deshabitado" is typical in that it relates thematically to Neruda's experience in the Orient. From the point of view of form, however, this prose poem, like the others of the second section, highlights the difference between Neruda's prose and poetry, especially his so-called prosaic verse. Contrasting the poet's use of these two literary forms, it is immediately apparent that for him the unique quality of prose was its continuity, the completeness of its expression, requiring logical closure. Thus, the effect in "El deshabitado" is heightened as the speaker refuses to speculate further, to continue to reason in a methodical fashion. Neruda's *Residencia* verse, on the other hand, in spite of its prosaic locutions, is more open, less bound in by logic, and utilizes an altogether unprosaic reasoning process based on implied and anticipated associations to complete the imagery. Whether prose or verse, the author is Pablo Neruda, and his artistic role is constant: to speak, to write, to record his special vision. Thus, his poems, all those in the first *Residencia,* stand as individual testimonials of moments of heightened awareness. The artist remains a visionary, but he does no more than record his discrete visions of the world in all its apparent chaos. In one poem, "Caballero solo" (Gentleman Alone), the speaker even refers to a "residencia solitaria" (solitary rooming house) where:

> seguramente, eternamente me rodea
> este gran bosque respiratorio y enredado
> con grandes flores como bocas y dentaduras
> y negras raíces en forma de uñas y zapatos.

> surely, eternally surrounds me this great forest respiratory and entwined with enormous flowers like mouths and teeth and black roots in the form of fingernails and shoes.

In this human forest the modern poet is as alone with himself as was the turn-of-the-century decadent in his ivory tower; both write because they must. To do otherwise would be to deny their vocation. Poetry is a calling and Neruda writes as one who has received the call. The reader can do little more than wonder why and how the poet writes and this apparently is his implied function in *Residencia en la tierra,* for it is only then that he can enter into the peculiar linguistic constructs of the poems themselves. For example, in "Arte poética" the poet does not deal with the art of composition as the title might suggest. Instead he presents an image of the artist at work, of the artist as a kind of sentinel, alert to the world and charged with capturing its every sign of life, no matter how vague or insignificant it may seem. Again, an absolute order and meaning are not to be imposed on this recorded experience:

> Entre sombra y espacio, entre guarniciones y doncellas,
> dotado de corazón singular y sueños funestos,
> precipitadamente pálido, marchito en la frente

y con luto de viudo furioso por cada día de vida
ay, para cada agua invisible que bebo soñolientamente
y de todo sonido que acojo temblando,
tengo la misma sed ausente y la misma fiebre fría,
un oído que nace, una angustia indirecta,
como si llegaran ladrones o fantasmas,
y en una cáscara de extensión fija y profunda,
como un camarero humillado, como una campana un poco
  ronca,
como un espejo viejo, como un olor de casa sola
en la que los huéspedes entran de noche perdidamente ebrios,
y hay un olor de ropa tirada al suelo, y una ausencia de flores,
posiblemente de otro modo aún menos melancólico,
pero, la verdad de pronto, el viento que azota mi pecho,
las noches de substancia infinita caídas en mi dormitorio,
el ruido de un día que arde con sacrificio
me piden lo profético que hay en mí, con melancolía,
y un golpe de objetos que llaman sin ser respondidos
hay, y un movimiento sin tregua, y un nombre confuso.

Between shadow and space, between garrisons and maidens, endowed with a singular heart and mournful dreams, precipitately pale, withered the face and with the mourning of a widower furious for each day of life, alas, for each invisible water that I drink sleepily and for every sound that I grasp trembling, I have the same absent thirst and the same cold fever, an ear that is born, an indirect anguish, as if thieves or ghosts were arriving, and in a shell of a fixed and profound extension, like a humiliated waiter, like a bell a bit cracked, like an old mirror, like the smell of a solitary house in which the roomers enter at night losingly drunk, and there is a smell of clothing tossed to the floor, and an absence of flowers, possibly in some other way even less melancholic, but, the truth suddenly, the wind that strikes my chest, the nights of infinite substance dropped in my bedroom, the noise of a day that burns with sacrifice they demand what is prophetic in me, with melancholy, and a crashing of objects which call without being answered there is, and a movement without pause, and a confused name.

The poem's internal confusion purports to be that of the modern world in which we live. The poet here is no less sensitive than his nineteenth-century counterpart, but he is no longer a visionary. He simply does not pretend to have a key to decipher the mystery of experience. And what is the role of the reader in this designedly hermetic system? As in the love poems, he still seems to be excluded. Here, as in *Tentativa del hombre infinito,* the lyric voice does not even pretend to be speaking to anyone, whether real or imaginary, but only to itself. Neruda's "Arte poética" reads like a catalog of doleful experience in which the extraordinarily sensitive perceiver ("dotado de corazón singular," endowed with a singular heart) is repeatedly and unexpectedly dismayed by what he sees and feels. A dramatic soliloquy, really an interior monologue organized as an enumerative series—note the repeated use of the conjunction "y" and its consequent accumulative force—the discourse is interrupted occasionally by a dissonant voice:

> y hay un olor de ropa tirada al suelo, y una ausencia de flores,
> *posiblemente de otro modo aún menos melancólico,*
> pero, la verdad de pronto, el viento que azota mi pecho,
> las noches de substancia infinita caídas en mi dormitorio,
> el ruido de un día que arde con sacrificio
> *me piden lo profético que hay en mí, con melancolía,*
> y un golpe de objetos que llaman sin ser respondidos
> hay, y un movimiento sin tregua, y un nombre confuso.

As in some of the cantos from *Tentativa,* the speaker, immersed in the free flow of the imagery, seems to be suddenly jolted into another plane of consciousness requiring yet another mode of discourse.

In *Veinte poemas de amor* we saw the efficacy of using a closed system of expression and were able to appreciate the unusual degree of intimacy it conveyed. This accomplishment, though, ultimately depended on the reader's acceptance of the sincerity of the lyric voice. *Residencia en la tierra,* on the other hand, is declamatory and even anti-lyrical. The basic discursive situation, although soliloquial as in the earlier poetry, does not seem to have the speaker filtering his sentiment, revising his expression. In this sense it is closer to *Tentativa del hombre infinito*. The change in Neruda's expressive system seems to have occurred almost immediately after the publication of *Veinte poemas de amor,* for in the earliest of the *Residencia* compositions, "Serenata," first published in 1925, we can already see the emergence of a certain anti-lyricism. The poem's somewhat overly traditional title leads the reader to expect a tender nocturnal love song, a serenade. And the poem's first lines even begin on this anticipated lyrical note, evoking the rosy countenance of the loved one. But midway through the strophe Neruda jars the reader's sensibility with an image of the lover coursing through the fields causing toads to scatter every which way:

> En tu frente descansa el color de las amapolas,
> el luto de las viudas halla eco, oh apiadada.
> Cuando corres detrás de los ferrocarriles en los campos,
> el delgado labrador te da la espalda,
> de tus pisadas brotan temblando los dulces sapos.

> On your face rests the color of poppies, the mourning of the widows finds an echo, oh poor thing. When you run behind the trains in the fields, the slim farmer turns his back to you, the sweet toads leap trembling from your steps.

The adjective "dulce," giving the unheard of image of sweet toads—not to mention the anti-pastoral railroad cars—underscores the calculated nature of this imagistic shock. The whole poem, in fact, seems to be organized around an anti-lyric principle. In the final strophe, the lonely lover keeps vigil "como un ladrón" (like a thief).

This anti-lyricism first emerged during Neruda's period of avant-garde experimentation; he developed it even further in the *Residencia* poetry. In "Tango del viudo" (Widower's Tango), a poem of 1929, we can begin to appreciate the lyrical qualities of the anti-lyric mode. Having left behind in Burma his native lover when he was transferred to Ceylon, Neruda writes a lament on her absence wherein certain elemental functions of the body (breathing and urinating) take on a powerfully evocative lyrical significance:

> Daría este viento de mar gigante por tu brusca respiración
> oída en largas noches sin mezcla de olvido,
> uniéndose a la atmósfera como el látigo a la piel del caballo.
> Y por oírte orinar, en la oscuridad, en el fondo de la casa,
> como vertiendo una miel delgada, trémula, argentina, obstinada,
> cuántas veces entregaría este coro de sombras que poseo

> I would give this gigantic sea wind for your brusque breathing heard in long nights without a mixture of forgetting,   uniting itself with the atmosphere like the whip on the horse's hide. And to hear you urinating, in the darkness, at the back of the house,   as though pouring out a fine honey, tremulous, silvery, obstinate,   how many times would I willingly give up this chorus of shadows that I possess.

In this and many other ways the first *Residencia* represents a significant departure from the lyric modality of *Veinte poemas de amor*. The distance between the two books is readily apparent. With *Tentativa* it is less so. Probably for this reason the publication of *Residencia en la tierra* in Santiago in 1933 prompted Chilean critics to contrast it with the love poems which had just been revised and republished the year before, although with one major and confusing variation: the original Poem IX, which began in a rather heavily wrought fashion, speaking of a "Fimbria rubia de un sol que no atardece nunca" (the golden hem of the never-setting sun), and ended with a delicate image comparing the poet's sadness to a ship at sea "atado por anclas de oro y seda" (tied down with anchors of silk and gold), was replaced with an entirely new composition whose initial strophe contains imagery decidedly within the new anti-lyrical mode of *Residencia en la tierra*:

Ebrio de trementina y largos besos,
estival, el velero de las rosas dirijo,
torcido hacia la muerte del delgado día,
cimentado en el sólido frenesí marino.

Heady with the smell of pine and long kisses, summery, I steer
the ship of roses, off-course toward the death of the slim day,
cemented in the solid frenzy of the sea.

The enigmatic opening of this poem and its curious reference
to "trementina" (turpentine, pine needles?) has prompted some
recent critics to contextually relate, albeit mistakenly, *Veinte
poemas de amor* with *Residencia en la tierra*. This is a poem of
1932, not 1924. But the fact that Neruda felt it necessary to
revise the love poems before republishing them, and to replace
the original Poem IX with a new composition, is an indication
of the poet's awareness of his own stylistic evolution, of his
passage from the delicate sentimentalism of his earlier work to
the assertive anti-lyricism of *Residencia en la tierra I*.

Residencia en la tierra II (1931–1935)

After publishing the limited edition of the first *Residencia*
in Santiago in 1933, Neruda was appointed Consul to Buenos
Aires, a post which put him in contact with a wider and much
more influential circle of writers and critics, including the
Spanish poet Federico García Lorca, then in Argentina also.
While there Neruda shared a speech (*al alimón*) with García
Lorca in the P.E.N. Club of Buenos Aires in which the two
poets stressed the new generation's debt to tradition as well as
the necessity to go beyond it. The following year, when Neruda
was transferred to Spain, García Lorca enthusiastically pre-
sented him as a unique new voice at his first public recital in
Madrid:

You are about to hear an authentic poet. One of those whose
senses are trained to a world that is not ours and that few people

perceive. A poet closer to death than to philosophy, closer to pain than to insight, closer to blood than to ink. A poet filled with mysterious voices that fortunately he himself does not know how to decipher . . . This is poetry that is not ashamed to break with tradition, that is not afraid of ridicule, and that can suddenly break out sobbing in the middle of the street.*

The Spanish poet is obviously describing the anguished existentialist author of the first *Residencia en la tierra*. But the Chilean's poetry had already undergone substantial change and the Spanish public would discover another Neruda, author of a poetry less dense, less introspective, and considerably more discursive, although equally "impure" and "unashamed." Neruda, perhaps because of his new and more public role as a reciter of his own poetry, had begun to experiment with a new diction. As the poet evolves, so also does his poetry; personal experience and public posture are one and the same.

Another poet, José Santos Chocano, has left an interesting testimonial concerning this linkage between the man and his work. Chocano, surviving dean of Spanish American Modernist poets in the thirties, and himself a master of the bombastic declamatory style, after attending a Neruda recital decided to write on the poet's unusual delivery:

> Pablo Neruda, hidden behind his mask of impassivity, begins a reading of his poems. His voice has a veiled nasality; his pronunciation is lazily dragged out; altogether his recitation gives an impression of languor and monotony. It seems to me that he prays his poems. In the same way that the faithful repeat their litanies, in a chorus that seems to rock and sway in sleep-inducing rhythms . . . The poet manages in his recital to infuse something of a liturgical emotion. My spiritual antennas vibrate picking up the messages of poetry as they are diffused throughout the atmosphere. Between the mask, each

* "Presentación de Pablo Neruda" (Madrid, December 6, 1934), Federico García Lorca, *Obras completas* (Madrid, Aguilar, 1964), p. 148.

poem and the manner in which it is recited, there is a mysterious harmony.*

What is surprising here is that Santos Chocano is describing a 1932 reading, and not of *Residencia en la tierra* but of *Veinte poemas de amor*. Evidently, Neruda's attitude toward his earlier poetry had changed; the tone of the love poems in this recital, like the text of Poem IX, had been totally updated. Something similar was to happen between the first and second *Residencia*. Where once the poet had been concentrated and introspective, he would later emerge as digressive and outward. It would seem that no sooner had he put the first *Residencia* behind him than that he was ready and able to express himself in a looser fashion, for in January of 1934 he published in Santiago's *El Mercurio* what must be his lightest poem since his student days, "Barcarola," a love-song whose varied free verse alone indicates the mature author's search for a new rhythmic principle based on a natural articulation. The title too is indicative of the more public nature of the poet's expression: the *barcarola* is the song of the Venetian gondoliers. The poem, which was incorporated into the second *Residencia* in 1935, is much too long to reproduce here in its entirety but an examination of the first strophe should suffice to give an idea of the fundamental change in diction. Verses of different length are used with great effectiveness to distribute rhythmically the many nuances of a single compound conditional phrase:

> Si solamente me tocaras el corazón,
> si solamente pusieras tu boca en mi corazón,
> tu fina boca, tus dientes,
> si pusieras tu lengua como una flecha roja
> allí donde mi corazón polvoriento golpea,
> si soplaras en mi corazón, cerca del mar, llorando,
> sonaría con un ruido oscuro, con sonido de ruedas de tren con
> sueño,

* José Santos Chocano, "Panorama lírico (a través de un recital poético)," *La Prensa* (Buenos Aires), March 12, 1933.

como aguas vacilantes,
como el otoño en hojas,
como sangre,
con un ruido de llamas húmedas quemando el cielo,
sonando como sueños o ramas o lluvias,
o bocinas de puerto triste,
si tú soplaras en mi corazón, cerca del mar,
como un fantasma blanco,
al borde de la espuma,
en mitad del viento,
como un fantasma desencadenado, a la orilla del mar llorando.

If you were only to touch my heart, if you were only to put your mouth on my heart, your fine mouth, your teeth, if you were to put your tongue like a red arrow there where my heart beats, if you were to whisper in my heart near the sea, crying, it would sound out with an obscure noise, with a sound of the wheels of a train with sleep, like wavering waters, like the autumn of leaves, like blood, with a noise of humid flames burning the sky, sounding out like dreams or frogs or rain, or horns of a sad port, if you were to whisper in my heart, near the sea, like a white phantom, on the edge of the spray, in the midst of the wind, like an unchained phantom, at the edge of the sea, crying.

The theme of love and absence is the same as in *Veinte poemas,* but gone is the morose and ponderous treatment of it. Here we have love poetry in a lighter, more public, vein. This is a poem to be spoken out loud, not to be read in silent solitude. If there is any overriding difference between the first two *Residencias,* it is one of tone: the difference between "decir" and "hablar," between saying and speaking, between describing an experience and relating it. For this reason perhaps the poems of the second *Residencia* seem to be more direct and outspoken, in a word, more oral.

If the volume of 1933 recorded somewhat existentially the chaos of the modern world and presented almost liturgically the poet's perception of its headlong rush toward extinction, of its daily dying, the volume of 1935 seems to be informed by a quite different attitude, one which implies that in spite of the fact that all things must die, life not only goes on, but it is not so bad after all. It could be better of course, but let us at least accept it as it is. Even the titles of certain poems like "No hay olvido" (There Is No Oblivion) and "Walking Around" convey immediately a new sense of accommodation. The anecdotal content as well as the narrative nature of these later compositions point to the fact that we are faced once more with the phenomenon of change. Neruda is creating yet another kind of poetry. In a composition like "No hay olvido," for example, the lyric voice is more self-conscious than in that of the earlier poetry. What is more, the poem is familiarly addressed not to an absent personage nor even to the poet's inner self, but frankly and refreshingly at last to us, his readers. As the discursive situation changes, Neruda would like us to forget all that metaphysical posturing of the past:

Si me preguntáis en dónde he estado
debo decir "Sucede."
Debo de hablar del suelo que oscurecen las piedras,
del río que durando se destruye:
no sé sino las cosas que los pájaros pierden,
el mar dejado atrás, o mi hermana llorando.
Por qué tantas regiones, por qué un día
se junta con un día? Por qué una negra noche
se acumula en la boca? Por qué muertos?

If you ask me where I have been I ought to say "It so happens." I ought to speak of the ground that is darkened by the stones, of the river that enduring destroys itself: I don't know anything more than the things that the birds lose, the sea left behind, or my sister crying. Why so many regions, why does one day join another day? Why does a black night gather in the mouth? Why dead people?

The questions are rhetorical and remain unanswered as in the first *Residencia;* here, though, the poem terminates with an invocation that no more such questions be asked:

> Pero no penetremos más allá de esos dientes,
> no mordamos las cáscaras que el silencio acumula,
> porque no sé qué contestar:
> hay tantos muertos,
> y tantos malecones que el sol rojo partía
> y tantas cabezas que golpean los buques,
> y tantas manos que han encerrado besos,
> y tantas cosas que quiero olvidar.

> But let's not penetrate beyond those teeth, let's not bite into the husks that silence accumulates, because I don't know what to answer: there are so many dead, and so many piers that the red sun was splitting and so many heads that beat against the ships and so many hands that have enclosed kisses, and so many things that I want to forget.

To forget, not to remember; to survive, not to philosophize; to write a poetry of the present, of the circumstantial here and now, of life not death—that is the new ambition. In "Walking Around," a poem whose carefully chosen English title suggests a certain aimlessness better than any Spanish equivalent might, we even find a stressed insistence on the boring quality of mere happenstance and the speaker's desire to break out of existential passivity through a sudden leap of the imagination:

> Sucede que me canso de ser hombre.
> Sucede que entro en las sastrerías y en los cines
> marchito, impenetrable, como un cisne de fieltro
> navegando en un agua de origen y ceniza.

> El olor de las peluquerías me hace llorar a gritos.
> Sólo quiero un descanso de piedras o de lana,
> sólo quiero no ver establecimientos ni jardines,
> ni mercaderías, ni anteojos, ni ascensores.

Sucede que me canso de mis pies y mis uñas
y mi pelo y mi sombra.
Sucede que me canso de ser hombre.

Sin embargo sería delicioso
asustar a un notario con un lirio cortado
o dar muerte a una monja con un golpe de oreja.
Sería bello . . .

It happens that I am tired of being a man. It happens that I
go into tailorshops and movies withered, impenetrable, like a
stuffed swan navigating in a water of origins and ashes.   The
smell of barbershops makes me cry out. I only want a rest of
stones or of wool, I only want not to see establishments or
gardens, or merchandise, or eyeglasses, or elevators.   It hap-
pens that I am tired of my feet and my nails and my hair and
my shadow. It happens that I am tired of being a man.   Yet,
it would be delightful to scare a notary with a cut lily, or to kill
a nun with a smack on the ear. It would be lovely . . .

Weary of what merely happens and desirous of entering more
fully into life's imaginative possibilities, the poet now speaks
directly and candidly to his reader, soliciting his complicity in
this new adventure. The discursive situation is not unlike that
of a traditional novel wherein the narrator speaks directly to
the reader, involving him in the imaginative construct.

More conscious than ever of his public readership, Neruda
seems to be striving for a more engaging style of discourse. And,
with regard to the later compositions of the second *Residen-
cia,* it is possible to speak of a kind of poetic realism, or, to be
more precise, an "unpoetic" realism. In the separate titles of
the "Cantos materiales," first published together in early 1935
to accompany the Spanish poets' homage to Neruda, this qual-
ity becomes most apparent: "Entrada a la madera," "Apogeo
del apio," and "Estatuto del vino" (Entrance to Wood, Apogee
of Celery, and Wine Ordinance).

Neruda's art, essentially experimental in nature, is rarely
programmatic; a new poetic modality, once found to be suc-

cessful in practice, is usually followed by an attempt on his part to explain it, to justify it aesthetically. Such was the case in 1924 with his public exegesis of the love poems, and, some eleven years later, the same thing would occur with the second *Residencia*. After *Veinte poemas de amor* Neruda's verse had taken a turn away from pure lyricism, toward a poetry of exalted personal experience, and had been gradually coming closer to a more direct and concrete literary expression in which a frank narrative modality would ultimately predominate. It is this later poetry that is so patently realistic and so obviously "impure." Thus, it is not surprising that shortly after the publication of the combined edition of *Residencia en la tierra* in September 1935 Neruda felt called upon to offer an explanation. And so in October of that same year, in the first issue of *Caballo Verde para la Poesía*, a new literary review he had just founded in Madrid, we find an essay-manifesto "Sobre una poesía sin pureza" (On an Impure Poetry), which seems designed to explain the new phoenomenon:

> It is very convenient, at certain times of the day or night, to observe deeply objects at rest: the wheels that have covered long, dusty distances, supporting heavy loads of vegetables or minerals, coal sacks, barrels, baskets, the handles and grips of the tools of a carpenter. The contact of man with the universe issues from these things like a lesson for the tortured lyric poet. The worn surfaces, the wear that hands have inflicted on things, the often tragic and always pathetic atmosphere of these objects infuses a kind of irresistible attraction for the reality of the world. The confused impurity of human beings is perceived in them, the grouping together, use and misuse of materials, footprints and fingerprints, the constancy of a human atmosphere inundating things from within and without. Thus should be the poetry we strive for, worn as though by acid from manual duties, penetrated by sweat and smoke, redolent of urine and lilies, and seasoned by the various professions that operate both within and outside the law.

The description is valid for almost all the *Residencia* poetry, from the immobile pulley wheel of "Galope muerto" to the elemental imagery of "Tango del viudo," valid even, as we shall see, for the later poetry of social commitment contained in *Tercera residencia*. Neruda, at this point in his development as a poet, is speaking out against the elitist attitude of later Modernism, against his earlier poetry of a "fimbria rubia de un sol que no atardece nunca" (the golden hem of the never-setting sun). The announced goal of impurity thus stands in sharp contrast to the refined writing of a Juan Ramón Jiménez or a Paul Valéry. In the context of such "pure poetry," the subject matter of the "Cantos materiales" is almost shocking in its ordinariness: wood, celery, and wine—not the ruby-like liquid of a crystal goblet, but the tavern swill of drunkards; in short, the real as opposed to the ideal, the everyday as opposed to the extraordinary. Or, as the poet himself somewhat prosily says in "Estatuto del vino":

> Hablo de cosas que existen. Dios me libre
> de inventar cosas cuando estoy cantando!

> I speak of things that exist. God deliver me from inventing
> things when I am singing!

Poetry is to be not only sincere but also uninvented, true, realistic. But, is a poem any less poetic or less literary because of this new realism? To inquire about the artistic worth of a song about wood, wine, or celery is to pose an aesthetic problem of another order, one not easy to resolve. With what can such poetry be compared? It seems to be without antecedent, to exist outside the literary tradition. Other poets had earlier composed odes to the simple things in life, but Neruda is doing much more than that. He is elevating the ordinary; he is giving a literary form to what is by definition not literary. In spite of its simple subject, wood, "Entrada a la madera" is essentially a mystic poem, written in the manner of the best religious poetry of the Spanish Golden Age. In this poetry the speaker, through a total abnegation of the senses, usually rises dreamily to a new intellectual level and, ultimately, to spiritual communion with God. In Neruda's poem, through a structured reversal of this procedure, the spiritual aspect is minimized and sensory perceptions are maximized as the speaker bodily falls down toward a physical union with earthly things:

> Con mi razón apenas, con mis dedos,
> con lentas aguas lentas inundadas,
> caigo al imperio de los nomeolvides,
> a una tenaz atmósfera de luto,
> a una olvidada sala decaída,
> a un racimo de tréboles amargos.

> With my reason scarcely, with my fingers, with slow waters slow inundations, I fall toward the realm of forget-me-nots, toward a tenacious atmosphere of mourning, toward a forgotten decayed room, toward a cluster of bitter clover.

What might at first seem to be a fall toward death is actually toward life. And, lest the reader miss the mystic allusion, an implied reference necessary to understand the poem's total meaning, the poet goes on to use imagery of inversion (sinking upward) and familiar religious symbols to present the vital union, not with God, but with matter, "sweet matter":

> Dulce materia, oh rosa de alas secas,
> en mi *hundimiento* tus pétalos *subo*
> con pies pesados de roja fatiga,
> y en tu catedral dura me arrodillo
> golpeándome los labios con un ángel. (emphasis mine)

> Sweet matter, oh rose of dry wings, in my sinking I climb up your petals with feet heavy with red fatigue, and in your hard cathedral I kneel bumping my lips against an angel.

Neruda establishes a mystic parallel and goes beyond it. In the love poems we saw how he first created a pattern of expectations only to violate it and jolt the reader into a new awareness. This is what he is again doing in these "Cantos materiales." The basic formula of mystic poetry is to describe spiritual communion in terms of sexual union. Neruda inverts this classic formula and describes an imagined physical communion with matter, with things. The emphatic references to fatigue, tired feet, kneeling in the hard cathedral, and the bumping of lips with a wooden statue combine to stress the corporeal quality, if not the uncontrolled nature of this hurtling fall toward materiality, this physical "entrance into wood," that is the real subject of the poem. In the final stanza all these diverse elements are fused together as though in a dream to create a strange atmosphere of physical spirituality, of bodily union with the cosmos. After a liturgical invocation to matter, exactly midway through the strophe, the speaker of "Entrada a la madera," not unlike a mystic or a sorcerer, conjures for union and then goes on to describe in realistic terms the desired harmony as though it were actually experienced:

> Poros, vetas, círculos de dulzura,
> peso, temperatura silenciosa,
> flechas pegadas a tu alma caída,
> seres dormidos en tu boca espesa,
> polvo de dulce pulpa consumida,
> ceniza llena de apagadas almas,
> *venid a mí, a mi sueño sin medida,*
> *caed en mi alcoba en que la noche cae*
> y cae sin cesar como agua rota,
> y a vuestra vida, a vuestra muerte asidme,
> y a vuestros materiales sometidos,
> a vuestras muertas palomas neutrales,
> y hagamos fuego, y silencio, y sonido,
> y ardamos, y callemos, y campanas.   (emphasis mine)

Pores, veins, circles of sweetness, weight, silent temperature, arrows stuck in your fallen soul, beings asleep in your dense mouth, power of sweet consumed pulp, ash filled with extinguished souls, come to me, to my limitless dream, fall into my bedroom in which the night falls and falls without stopping like broken water, and to your life, to your death bind me, and to your subdued materials, and to your dead neutral doves, and let's make fire, and silence, and sound, and let's flame up, and be silent, and bells.

Neruda's technique in the concluding verses merits further comment. He first establishes a noun pattern ("fuego," "silencio," "sonido"), followed by a parallel, but incomplete, verb pattern: "ardamos, y callemos, y campanas." By substituting the noun "campanas" for the anticipated verb ("campanear," to ring), a most forceful closure is obtained, freezing the poem's action and crystallizing its meaning. What better way to illustrate the materiality of this calculatedly impure poetry?

The poet's stance, his insertion of himself as a personage in these "Cantos materiales," as in other poems of the second *Residencia,* is also noteworthy. Not simply an individual consciousness (as in *Tentativa* and the love poems), nor an impassive recorder of life's waning processes (as in the first *Residencia*), he is a sounding board, a voice for what is voiceless. The poem on celery concludes with an articulated image of this newly assumed role:

Fibras de oscuridad y luz llorando,
ribetes ciegos, energías crespas,
río de vida y hebras esenciales,
verdes ramas de sol acariciado,
aquí estoy, en la noche, escuchando secretos,
desvelos, soledades,
y entráis, en medio de la niebla hundida,
hasta crecer en mí, hasta comunicarme
la luz oscura y la rosa de la tierra.

Fibers of darkness and weeping light, blind grooves, curly energies, river of life and essential threads, green branches of caressed sun, here I am, in the night, listening to secrets, wakefulness, solitudes, and you all enter, amid the sunken cloud, until you grow in me, until you communicate to me the dark light and the rose of the earth.

The second *Residencia* departs from the first in terms of diction, of the spoken quality of its poetic expression. Yet, because both volumes were published at the same time, in 1935, with the two-part Cruz y Raya edition, they have been considered ever since as an interrelated, even integral, work. Critics at the time, dazzled by the revolutionary quality of this poetry, failed to notice much difference between the two volumes. To this day there is a tendency to consider all these poems together, overlooking even the authorial indication of chronology contained in both the internal arrangement of the texts and in the external dating: the first volume carries the subtitle 1925–1931; the second 1931–1935. The popular Losada edition of *Residencia en la tierra* today includes both in a single volume as did the first English translation (Angel Flores, New Directions, 1946). This grouping principle is now so firmly established that the most recent translation (Donald Walsh, New Directions, 1973) includes *Tercera residencia* (1935–1945) as well. Why have Neruda's publishers and translators insisted on viewing twenty years of assorted poems as an integral whole? The fact is that, in spite of the many and obvious differences among these three volumes, there is a nucleus of poetry that can logically be considered to constitute a *Residencia* cycle.

Thus far, in order to show the uniqueness of Neruda's work at various stages of his development, I have stressed the more obvious differences between the first two *Residencias*. But there are also similarities. The spoken diction so characteristic of the second *Residencia* is anticipated in at least one poem of the first, "Ritual de mis piernas" (Ritual of My Legs):

Largamente he permanecido mirando mis largas piernas,
con ternura infinita y curiosa, con mi acostumbrada pasión,
como si hubieran sido las piernas de una mujer divina,

profundamente sumida en el abismo de mi tórax:
y es que, la verdad, cuando el tiempo, el tiempo pasa,
sobre la tierra, sobre el techo, sobre mi impura cabeza,
y pasa, el tiempo pasa, y en mi lecho no siento de noche que una
   mujer está respirando, durmiendo, desnuda y a mi lado,
entonces . . .

For a long time I have remained looking at my long legs, with infinite and curious tenderness, with my accustomed passion, as though they had been the legs of a divine woman profoundly sunk in the abyss of my thorax: and the fact is that when time, when time passes, over the earth, over the roof, over my impure head, and it passes, time passes, and in my bed at night I do not feel a woman is breathing, sleeping, naked alongside of me, then . . .

The difference actually is in the tone, which derives from the internal organization of the verse. The poetic line, lengthy and punctuated so as to be halting and repetitious, makes this 1930 poem more weighty, more solemn, than, say, "Walking Around." Both texts do, however, share a certain spoken quality.

Other similarities between one *Residencia* and another are thematic, mostly because Neruda's poetic perspective is so intensely personal. It is possible to view the frank sexuality of the poems of the third section of the 1935 book—"Oda con un lamento," "Material nupcial," "Agua sexual" (Ode with a Lament, Nuptial Material, and Sexual Water)—in the context of the *Claridad* program and the earlier love poetry. For example, "Material nupcial" is nothing less than a first-person description of the sex act. It begins in this uninhibited way:

De pie como un cerezo sin cáscara ni flores,
especial, encendido, con venas y saliva,
y dedos y testículos,
miro una niña de papel y luna,
horizontal, temblando y respirando y blanca
y sus pezones como dos cifras separadas,

y la rosal reunión de sus piernas en donde
su sexo de pestañas nocturnas parpadea.

Standing like a cherry tree without bark or flowers, special,
burning hot, with veins and saliva, and fingers and testicles, I
look at a girl of paper and moon, horizontal, trembling and
breathing and white and her nipples like two separate ciphers,
and the rosy meeting of her legs where her sex of nocturnal
eyelashes winks.

Again though there is an important difference: gone is the
lyricism, the tender erotic quality of the earlier love poems.
What we have here is a more direct, less impassioned treatment
of sex.

Similarities—and dissimilarities—of form and content not-
withstanding, the fundamental linkage between these two
books is chronological, containing as they do, almost all the
poetry composed between 1925 and 1935. In this scheme the
one constant element is Neruda himself, perpetually dissatis-
fied with what he has accomplished, ever ready to begin anew.
For this reason, when traced chronologically, his variegated
styles may be seen to be a constantly evolving function of his
changing personal and artistic circumstances.

In all the poems of the *Residencia* cycle, a certain attention
to chronology is important, since the order of occurrence can,
and often does, reveal a direction as well as a pattern of
change. In the study of literature such patterns are not always
easy to discern, for authors either inadvertently or intention-
ally mislead their readers. Neruda is no exception. The inac-
curate 1931 and 1935 cutoff dates he gave for *Residencia* I and
II are examples. The first volume contains many poems pub-
lished after 1931; the second contains none published before
1934. The date 1931 actually corresponds to Neruda's depar-
ture from the Far East; placed on the 1933 book, it was meant
to imply that the poems contained therein correspond to this
singular experience.

In 1932, marking his return to the Hispanic world, Neruda

had himself photographed in the swirling robes of a swami, as if to suggest that he had "gone native." He was propagating the myth of his exotic acculturation, so it is not surprising that his earliest readers came to interpret the striking hermeticism of his poetry in equally exotic ways. Some critics have made far too much of Neruda's isolation, of his lack of contact with Spanish speakers, even of his plea to his friends to send him a Spanish dictionary. All these circumstances are undoubtedly true, but it is no less true that the peculiar density of the early *Residencia* poetry also derives from the author's projected literary image of himself. On this point his letters to Héctor Eandi and González Vera are remarkably similar in tone and content.

Neruda's poetry at this time, like his public image of himself, is a carefully constructed artifice. And so it should be. A 1929 poem "Monzón de junio" (June Monsoon), poetizing the eery moment of calm before the cyclical monsoon winds—blowing six months one way and six the other—change direction, would have its title changed to "Monzón de mayo" (May Monsoon) when collected in *Residencia en la tierra* in 1933. The euphony of the alliteration is artistically more important to the poet than factual accuracy. What is more, "Galope muerto" was written and published in Chile in 1926, long before Neruda ever imagined he would be sent to Rangoon.

What is true for the first book of the *Residencia* cycle is also true for the second. Its spoken diction corresponds to another, newly assumed literary role: public reciter; the poet on Olympus, chatting familiarly with the gods. This is the attitude informing the "Cantos materiales." It is also the pose directly taken up in the ode to García Lorca:

> Ven a que te corone, joven de la salud
> y de la mariposa, joven puro
> como un negro relámpago perpetuamente libre,
> y conversando entre nosotros,
> ahora, cuando no queda nadie entre las rocas,
> hablemos sencillamente como eres tú y soy yo:
> para qué sirven los versos si no es para el rocío?

Come let me crown you youth of health, and the butterfly, pure youth like a black bolt of lightning perpetually free, and conversing among ourselves, now, when no one is left among the rocks, let us speak simply as you are and so am I: of what use are verses if not for the dew?

The world changes, Neruda's perception of his place in the world changes, and these circumstantial shifts are ultimately reflected in his poetry. In this context, no change was more dramatic, more far-reaching in its human and literary implications than that deriving from his residence in Spain during the early days of the Spanish Civil War.

Tercera residencia (1935–1945)

The third and last volume of the *Residencia* cycle, like the other two, is essentially a collection of poems arranged in sections (five), distributed chronologically. The first two sections seem to continue the thematic concerns of *Residencia en la tierra II*. One poem, "Las furias y las penas" (Furies and Sorrows), whose title contains an allusion to Quevedo, was first published as a separate item in Santiago in 1939; according to the author's note it was actually composed much earlier, before the war:

This poem was written in 1934. How many things have come to pass since then! Spain, where I wrote it, is a girdle of ruins. Ah, if only with a drop of poetry or of love we were able to placate the anger of the world, but that can only be done through combat and a determined will. The world has changed, and my poetry with it. A drop of blood spilled on these lines will remain forever alive on them, indelible like love.

The author thus draws attention to the fact that his poetry has changed with the times. It is not surprising, therefore, that what is new and innovative—not to say controversial—in

89

Tercera residencia is found in the later poetry, that which is contained in the last three, significantly titled, sections: "Reunión bajo las nuevas banderas," "España en el corazón," "Canto a Stalingrado" (Meeting under New Flags, Spain in My Heart, Song to Stalingrad).

The collection, first published by Losada in 1947, contains the literary record of a decade (1935–1945), the most important transitional period in Neruda's development as a poet. Nonetheless, it is the least studied and most maligned of the three *Residencia* volumes. Variously condemned as propagandistic or, what is worse, unpoetic, this book deserves much more careful attention than it has received to date. The original charge regarding its supposedly unpoetic quality is the most ludicrous and today requires only a reading of the poems to be set aside. Since *Crepusculario* (1923) Neruda had steadily expanded the domain of his poetry by incorporating into it subjects previously considered unfit. He simply continued to do this in *Tercera residencia,* whose principal themes—war and politics, ranging from the Spanish Civil War to the Second World War, from Bolívar to contemporary liberators—no longer seem so unorthodox today as they once did. As for propaganda, that charge is the most gratuitous since these poems for the most part were written to advance specific causes, to spread certain ideas, to propagate. In the broadest sense of the word, advertising is propaganda. So also is the work of missionaries. And the poems of *Tercera residencia* are like pamphlets written with an almost missionary zeal for causes which, while once perhaps controversial, are now merely a part of contemporary history.

The fact that many of the *Tercera residencia* poems were originally created as a kind of propaganda does not automatically make them less literary. The only real difference is one of criterion; these literary constructs must be judged not on the basis of some abstract ideal of beauty, but effectiveness. Thematically outside the literary tradition, they make use of traditional literary form to achieve a certain effect: to persuade. Since the content of each poem is inextricably linked to a particular time and place, an attention to chronology is paramount. Only by placing each major piece in its proper historical context can we appreciate Neruda's total artistic achievement over the ten-year period defined by the poems of *Tercera residencia.*

A historical context implies a cultural context as well. And while the political lesson Spain offered Neruda in the 1930s would be important for the development of his social consciousness, so also would its literary ambiance have an effect on his evolving poetic practice. The Spanish writers of Lorca's generation had just begun to rediscover, almost with a vengeance, certain neglected authors of the baroque period. While the avant-garde in the 1920s was pleased with itself for being able to appreciate the formal perfection of a Góngora, the more committed writers of the thirties would find in the radical audacity of a Quevedo a more complete literary model. Neruda, upon arriving in Madrid, participated in this general trend of revaluation of the Spanish baroque. In 1935 he even prepared a selection of Quevedo for the Catholic literary review *Cruz y Raya* (the same enterprise that published the combined edition of his *Residencia en la tierra*); he also prefaced an edition of yet another seventeenth-century revival, the Conde de Villamediana. This renewed attention to the great literature of the past was to have an effect on the form and content of Neruda's own poetry. Not uncharacteristically, he would eventually detail the circumstances of the changes in his work; and in a radio speech of 1939 ("Quevedo adentro," Quevedo Within), he publicly acknowledged not only his admiration for the great Spanish poet, but also the catalytic effect the belated discovery had on his personal outlook, moving him from an attitude of anguished despair to a kind of social optimism. What most fascinated Neruda—besides Quevedo's condemnation of corruption, his civic spirit, and his intense passion for love and life—was his notion of "la agricultura de la muerte," the cultivation of death:

For Quevedo metaphysics is immensely physical . . . If on being born we begin to die, if each day brings us closer to an already determined limit, if life itself is a pathetic stage of death, if the very instant of budding forth advances toward the decay of which the final moment is only the culmination of its passage, aren't we integrated with death in our daily life, aren't we a perpetual part of death, aren't we then the most audacious part, the part that has already left death? Isn't the most mortal thing also the most vital? For this reason, in such an uncertain matter, Quevedo gave me a clear biology lesson. Not that we pass through life in vain, not Ecclesiastes, nor Kempis, mere adornments of necrology, but the advanced key to life. If we have already died, if we have just come from a profound crisis, we can lose our fear of death. If the giant step of death is birth, the tiniest step of life is death. Life is actually enriched by Quevedo as I read him, because Quevedo has been for me not just a text, but a lived experience.*

The poetry of Quevedo was an important influence on Neruda midway through the *Residencia* cycle. So was the Spanish Civil War. Completely setting behind him the hermetic inwardness of his earlier literature, he begins to speak out for life in the poems of *Tercera residencia;* he begins to voice societal concerns with the vigor of a pamphleteer and the conviction of a missionary. His new faith is in man, in mankind. The voice of the poet is no longer singular, that of an individual alone and adrift in an alien world; rather he is a part of society. He presumes to speak now not only for himself but also for others. The experience of Spain, culturally and politically, had transformed him. Revitalized by Quevedo and radicalized by the Spanish Civil War, he became politically outspoken. In a 1937 interview he had this to say regarding his outlook as a socially committed writer: "I am not a Communist. Nor a Socialist. Nor anything. I am simply a writer. A free writer who loves freedom. I love the people. I belong to

* "Viaje al corazón de Quevedo," *Obras completas* (Buenos Aires, Losada, 1968), II, 14.

the people because I am one of them. That is why I am anti-fascist. My adhesion to the people is not tainted with orthodoxy nor submission."* The new posture assumed is that of a radical nonconformist. *Tercera residencia* must, therefore, be considered in this light, from the dual perspective of art and society, poetry and politics.

Such a perspective is absolutely necessary for a total appreciation of the major compositions of *Tercera residencia,* especially for "España en el corazón," a multisectioned poem of some eight hundred verses on the deepfelt tragedy of a people at war. Originally published as a separate volume in Chile in 1937, it was reprinted the following year in Spain by the Spanish Republican Army with the following dedicatory note:

> The great poet Pablo Neruda (the most profound voice of America since Rubén Darío, as García Lorca once said) lived among us during the first few months of the war. Later, at sea, as though from exile, he wrote the poems of this book. The Commissariat of the Eastern Division now reprints it in Spain. Soldiers of the Republic made the paper, set the type, and operated the press. May the poet receive this as a dedication.

The Republicans find that Neruda's poem speaks for their cause. Neruda, on the other hand, realizes that the poetry of "España en el corazón" is so radically different from everything he had done thus far that in the text of the poem itself he offered an explanation. In a section appropriately subtitled "Explico algunas cosas" (I Explain a Few Things) he speaks rhetorically of the circumstances of his literary transformation:

> Preguntaréis: Y dónde están las lilas?
> Y la metafísica cubierta de amapolas?
> Y la lluvia que a menudo golpeaba

* Interview in *Ercilla* (Santiago), November 12, 1937, p. 11. Eight years later, in 1945, as the Second World War was drawing to a close, Neruda joined the Chilean Communist Party.

sus palabras llenándolas
de agujeros y pájaros?

Os voy a contar todo lo que me pasa.

Yo vivía en un barrio
de Madrid...

You will ask: And where are the lilacs? And the metaphysics
covered over with poppies? And the rain that often would beat
his words filling them with holes and birds? I am going to tell
you everything that happens to me. I used to live in a section
of Madrid . . .

The poet is now a protagonist in his own story, the real story
of his personal quest for meaning and of the different literary
stages which marked his progress. Having passed beyond the
lyric modality of his love poetry, beyond the meditative mode
of his earlier *Residencia* poetry, he speaks directly of what he,
Pablo Neruda, has witnessed in Spain.

The poet's new role is that of a chronicler, not unlike that
of the medieval jongleur, and the conversational diction tried
out so successfully in some of the later *Residencia* poems is
here used to even greater advantage inasmuch as the discursive
situation is now openly recitative. The vocal style turns out to
be rhythmically free and declamatory as the poem continues:

Yo vivía en un barrio
de Madrid, con campanas,
con relojes, con árboles.

Desde allí se veía
el rostro seco de Castilla
como un océano de cuero.

                 Mi casa era llamada

la casa de las flores, porque por todas partes
estallaban geranios: era
una bella casa
con perros y chiquillos.

                    Raúl, te acuerdas?

Te acuerdas, Rafael?
>Federico, te acuerdas

debajo de la tierra,
te acuerdas de mi casa con balcones en donde
la luz de junio ahogaba flores en tu boca?

I used to live in a section of Madrid, with bells, with clocks, with trees. From there one could see the dried-out face of Castille like an ocean of leather. My house was called the house of flowers, because everywhere there burst forth geraniums: it was a beautiful house with dogs and children. Raúl, do you remember? Do you remember, Rafael? Federico, do you remember under the earth, do you remember my house with balconies where the light of June would smother the flowers in your mouth?

In lyric poetry the problem is to convince the reader of the sincerity of the sentiment expressed. Here, the problem is rather different: to persuade the reader of the truth, the factuality of what is being narrated. Neruda employs an interesting authenticating device. We readers, to whom the poem is now expressly directed, are made to feel part of a much larger group; we are included in the literary circle of the poet and his friends. As Neruda relates the details of his personal experience he asks this other audience to verify the accuracy of what he has to say. The fact that we know that Federico (García Lorca), Raúl (González Tuñón), and Rafael (Alberti) are victims of the war, either dead or in exile, contributes to our tacit acceptance of their silence. The rhetorical questions addressed to them are rendered especially forceful by a combination of new and traditional devices. The free verses of varied length correspond to the natural rhythmic pulse of the declamatory phrase, while the displaced margins, a traditional device of classical verse drama, are used to mark time, to measure a pause that is pregnant with meaning. Silence in this way becomes a signifying presence of assent. Neruda's personal story is thus made part of a larger community of interests. Being less unique it is more universal. His experience is made to stand for that of Spain; his radicalization that of the Spanish people. Both are the innocent victims of a senseless war. In this view the villain is fascism, personified by the forces of Franco.

Partisan poetry, to be effective (persuasive), must establish a system of crossovers between the personal and the universal. Not to do so is to be merely tendentious. In "España en el corazón" Neruda creates these crossovers by skillfully resorting to a variety of diverse techniques. In "Explico algunas cosas" he details the destruction of his house, his neighborhood and the idyllic existence they represented for him and his friends. What is unique and particular is made general and universal in a subsequent section, "Cómo era España" (What Spain Was Like), through an evocative enumeration of other villages and towns. A kaleidoscope of remote victims emerges:

> Piedra solar, pura entre las regiones
> del mundo, España recorrida
> por sangres y metales, azul y victoriosa,
> proletaria de pétalos y balas, única
> viva y soñolienta y sonora.
>
> Huélamo, Carrascosa,
> Alpedrete, Buitrago,
> Palencia, Argenda, Galve,
> Galapagar, Villalba.
>
> Peñarrubia, Cedrillas,
> Alcocer, Tamurejo,
> Aguadulce, Pedrera,
> Fuente Palmera, Colmenar, Sepúlveda . . .

> Ancestral stone, pure among the regions of the world, Spain crisscrossed by blood and metal, blue and victorious, proletarian of buds and bullets, unique alive and dreamy and sonorous   Huélamo, Carrascosa . . .

This torrent of rustic place names continues for some fifty more lines. The lengthy enumeration of the unfamiliar is meant to tax the reader's patience and in doing so to overwhelm him with the extent of the tragedy. The particular is made universal through accumulation. Neruda's singular experience is thus multiplied.

The purpose of "España en el corazón" is twofold: to chronicle the author's experience and to persuade his readers to share his interpretation of that same experience. Fundamental to the rhetoric of persuasion is the device of repetition. For this reason, "Explico algunas cosas" closes with a studied variation of the rhetorical question with which it began:

> Preguntaréis por qué su poesía
> no nos habla del sueño, de las hojas,
> de los grandes volcanes de su país natal?
>
> Venid a ver la sangre por las calles.
> Venid a ver
> la sangre por las calles,
> venid a ver la sangre
> por las calles!

You will ask why does his poetry not speak to us of dreams, of the leaves, of the great volcanoes of his native land?   Come and see the blood in the streets. Come and see the blood in the streets, come and see the blood in the streets!

The original question was concerned with style, the variant with theme. The answer to both is given in the form of an example, a thrice-repeated command to witness what the poet has witnessed in all its complexity. Versification is an important modulating device here as the command first stated in the elevated measure of the noble hendecasyllable, Spain's renaissance verse ("Venid a ver la sangre por las calles"), is recast more urgently as a curt tetrasyllable ("Venid a ver"), followed, ironically, by a lyric heptasyllable, the combining verse of the ode ("la sangre por las calles"). When recombined for the third and last time, the resulting heptasyllabic invitation is macabre

("Venid a ver la sangre"), especially when it is followed by the exclamatory finale ("por las calles!"). The procedure is simple, but the effect is complex, particularly if the poem is read aloud, as it is meant to be.

This is poetry in the oral style. *Tercera residencia,* taken as a whole, indicates the extent of Neruda's transition—from the written soliloquial mode of *Veinte poemas de amor* ("Puedo *escribir* los versos más tristes . . ."—I can write the saddest verses) to the present declamatory style ("Os voy a *contar"*—I am going to tell you). The danger with a completely oral diction is that the composition will not be treated as a poem, but as mere speech, the transcription of discourse. The advantage of poetry is that the reader is conditioned to react to it differently, more intensely. Neruda, in "España en el corazón" retains this advantage by signaling the reader on occasion with the most noticeable forms of traditional poetic expression: rhymed stanzas and metered verses. In one section of the poem, the villains, Franco and his generals, are dramatically envisioned in hell. Appropriately, the verse form employed is that of Dante's *Divine Comedy,* the *terza rima.* "Mola en los infiernos" (Mola in Hell) symbolically poetizes a 1937 news item, the plane crash in which the insurrectionist general was killed:

> Es arrastrado el turbio mulo Mola
> de precipicio en precipicio eterno
> y como va el naufragio de ola en ola,
> desbaratado por azufre y cuerno,
> cocido en cal y hiel y disimulo,
> de antemano esperado en el infierno,
> va el infernal mulato, el Mola mulo
> definitivamente turbio y tierno
> con llamas en la cola y en el culo.

Dragged is the turbid Mola mule from cliff to eternal cliff and as the shipwrecked man goes from wave to wave, routed by brimstone and horn, cooked in lime and bile and deceit, already

expected in hell, goes the infernal mulatto, the mule Mola
definitively turbid and tender, with flames on his tail and up
his ass.

The combination of interlaced end rhyme (ABA, BCB, CBC)
and the alliterative, internally rhymed hendecasyllables echoes
on the ear, stressing in the process a play on words not normally
given literary treatment: "Mola–mulo," "cola–culo."

"España en el corazón," because of this unusual combination
of cultivated form and newsreel content, offended the sensibil-
ities of some critics only just beginning to accustom themselves
to the more subtle reading required by Neruda's earlier her-
meticism. The brutal terminology of war was in fact more
disturbing to many in 1937 than the scatological vocabulary so
exquisitely employed in the first two *Residencias*. But war is
brutal and the purpose of the poem was to impress the reader
with just that fact. So, in 1937, as Neruda's poetry became a
kind of propaganda, he publicly began to cultivate a style of
expression designed to move the reader totally, to affect not
only his literary sensibility but his social consciousness as well.
The result was a poetry that when it failed to persuade could
only provoke.

And provoke it did. There is a pair of war poems which,
caused something of a scandal in 1942–43. At that time Stalin-
grad was under siege by the Nazis. Neruda then wrote two
songs to Stalingrad. Both are included in *Tercera residencia*.
The first, "Canto a Stalingrado," was originally published in
Mexico City as a poster and, were it not for the controversy it
caused, would perhaps be scarcely remembered. Although
written mostly in unrhymed alexandrines, it has the easy nar-
rative flow of a "romance," the traditional Spanish ballad. A
time-honored procedure of the ballad is to treat in a lyric-
narrative style the conflict between Moorish- and Christian-
held parts of medieval Spain. Often the coveted places were
personified and sometimes even dialogued coquettishly with

the poem's principal speaker. Neruda's 1942 composition relies on this tradition to give literary form to his concern with the fate of a beleaguered Russian city:

> Ciudad, estrella roja, dicen el mar y el hombre,
> ciudad, cierra tus rayos, cierra tus puertas duras,
> cierra, ciudad, tu ilustre laurel ensangrentado,
> y que la noche tiemble con el brillo sombrío
> de tus ojos detrás de un planeta de espadas.
>
> Y el español recuerda Madrid y dice: hermana,
> resiste, capital de la gloria, resiste.
>   .   .   .   .
> Ella conoce la soledad, España,
> como hoy, Stalingrado, tú conoces la tuya.
> España desgarró la tierra con sus uñas
> cuando París estaba más bonita que nunca.
> España desangraba su inmenso árbol de sangre
> cuando Londres peinaba . . .

City, red star, say the man and the sea, city, shut down your rays of light, close your strong doors, take down, city, your illustrious laurel now bloodied, and let the night tremble with the dark glow of your eyes behind a planet of swords. And the Spaniard remembers Madrid and says: sister, resist, capital of glory, resist . . . She knows her loneliness, Spain, as today, Stalingrad, you know yours. Spain tore at the earth with her nails when Paris was lovelier than ever. Spain was bleeding her immense tree of blood when London was grooming . . .

The poem, like its traditional antecedent, has an elegant simplicity and is conventional in every way, save one: the name of the city poetized—Stalingrad. A five-syllable mouthful in Spanish, because of the prosthetic "e," this word, *Es-ta-lin-gra-do,* stuck in the throat of many readers in 1942. Demonstrations were organized against Neruda's violation of Mexican neutrality (he was then Chile's consul to México) and the poem was roundly condemned as partisan propaganda, which of course it was. The tender lyricism accorded to Stalin's namesake persuaded few and provoked many, and Neruda was forced to leave México. Before departing, he composed another poem, designed this time not only to persuade but also to provoke. He chose the classic hendecasyllable for a "Nuevo canto de amor a Stalingrado" (New Love Song to Stalingrad):

> Yo escribí sobre el tiempo y sobre el agua,
> describí el luto y su metal morado,
> yo escribí sobre el cielo y la manzana,
> ahora escribo sobre Stalingrado.

> I wrote about weather and water, I described mourning and its purple character, I wrote about the sky and the apple, now I write about Stalingrad.

And so it goes for another twenty-seven strophes, the rhyme scheme remaining constant in the second and fourth verses, thus pounding into the reader's mind twenty-seven more times the name of *Stalingrado.*

Political poetry can be short-lived. When the circumstances which inspired it lose their timeliness, the poem loses its vigor. Today Stalin is a bad memory, Stalingrad is no more, and this poem with its powerful end-rhyme is a relic of the past. But not all of Neruda's *Tercera residencia* poems are so frozen in time. And even those which are contain an enduring message of love, of optimism and faith in man's future expressed in a timeless literary form. One of the more moving war-poems concerns Germany; "Canto a los ríos de Alemania" (Song to the Rivers of Germany) is a poem not of hate for the arch-enemy, but of love for its victimized people. It seems to say that when the winter of war is over, the spring thaw will bring life to the nation; the rivers of life will flow once again in a new Germany. The message is simple, even simplistic. But it is powerful and persuasive due to the literary form which conveys it, the *ronda,* a children's school song whose didactic effectiveness depends on the principle of transformation through varied repetition:

Sobre el Rhin, en la noche, lleva el agua una boca
y la boca una voz y la voz una lágrima
y una lágrima corre por todo el Rhin dorado
donde ya la dulzura de Lorely no vive,
una lágrima empapa las cepas cenicientas
para que el vino tenga también sabor de lágrimas.
Sobre el Rhin, en la noche, lleva el agua una lágrima,
una voz, una boca que lo llena de sal.

On the Rhine, at night, the water carries a mouth and the
mouth a voice and the voice a tear and a tear flows all along the
golden Rhine where the sweetness of Lorelei no longer lives,
a tear soaks through the ashen vines so that the wine may also
have a taste of tears. On the Rhine, at night, the water carries
a tear, a voice, a mouth that fills it with salt.

The Rhine, the Oder, and the Elbe each in turn thaws, bring-
ing new life to the heart of Germany. The poem closes on this
soberly didactic note:

Un nuevo río corre profundo y poderoso
desde tu torturado corazón, Alemania,
y desde la desdicha sus aguas se levantan.
Lo voz secreta crece junto a las rojas márgenes
y el hombre sumergido se levanta y camina.

A new river flows deep and powerful from your tortured heart,
Germany, and from misfortune its waters rise. The secret voice
grows next to the red banks and the submerged man gets up and
walks.

In the poems of *Tercera residencia* Neruda rediscovers the
expressive potential of traditional poetic forms. Rather than
continue to labor toward the perfection of a style so uniquely
personal that his phrases literally drip with himself, as he once
said of the first *Residencia,* Neruda now is more concerned that
his poetry be effective, that it reach his reader in the most
direct way possible. To write against tradition is to overlook

the fact that the reader comes to a poem from within tradition. For this reason, in a poetry which pretends to persuade rather than record, the poet must adjust his expression to suit the audience and the occasion. Thus, in an official recital at the University of Mexico in 1941 commemorating the anniversary of the death of Bolívar, Neruda makes use of explicit allusion. His "Canto para Bolívar" (Song for Bolívar), composed for the occasion, is patterned on the Lord's Prayer:

> Padre nuestro que estás en la tierra, en el agua, en el aire
> de toda nuestra extensa latitud silenciosa,
> todo lleva tu nombre, padre, en nuestra morada:
> tu apellido la caña levanta a la dulzura,
> el estaño bolívar tiene un fulgor bolívar,
> el pájaro bolívar sobre el volcán bolívar,
> la patata, el salitre, las sombras especiales,
> las corrientes, las vetas de fosfórica piedra,
> todo lo nuestro viene de tu vida apagada,
> tu herencia fueron ríos, llanuras, campanarios,
> tu herencia es el pan nuestro de cada día, padre.

> Our Father who art in earth, in water, in the air of all our immense and silent latitude, all bears thy name, father in our land: thy name the sugar raises to its sweetness, Bolivar tin has a Bolivar brightness, the Bolivar bird over the Bolivar volcano, the potato, nitrate, special shadows, the currents, the veins of phosphoric stone, all that is ours comes from thine extinguished life, thy heritage was rivers, plains, bell towers, thy heritage is this our daily bread, Father.

This poem, whose opening strophe is so clear and straightforward, so publicly recitative, has a density of expression not unlike that of the earlier hermetic poetry. Its eleven lengthy verses form a single run-on phrase, enumerative and accumulative. There is a difference though. Whereas before Neruda practiced a kind of chaotic enumeration, here everything named has an integral place not only in the poem, but in the poetized cosmos of America, the New World sacrificially created by Bolívar. Death is life, our daily bread. The rush for extinction of, say, "Galope muerto" is finally transformed into a paean to life, to continued meaningful existence. What Neruda learned from Quevedo, the metaphysics of "la agricultura de la muerte," is now an integral part of his poetic system. Death leads to life.

"Canto para Bolívar" is doubly important for, while it completes the *Residencia* cycle, it also signals a new direction in the poet's thematic concerns. Politicized in war-torn Europe, Neruda in post-revolutionary Mexico—the Mexico of the murals of Rivera, Orozco, and Siqueiros—discovers the possibilities of America as subject for his new poetry of commitment. The Spanish experience is brought home to the New World. The prayer to Bolívar has an epilogue, a personal note directed straight to the audience:

> Yo conocí a Bolívar una mañana larga,
> en Madrid, en la boca del Quinto Regimiento,
> Padre, le dije, eres o no eres o quién eres?
> Y mirando el Cuartel de la Montaña, dijo:
> "Despierto cada cien años cuando despierta el pueblo."

> I came upon Bolívar one endless morning, in Madrid, in the mouth of the Fifth Column, Father, I said to him, are you or are you not, or who are you? And, looking at the Montaña Barracks, he said: "I awake every hundred years when the people awake."

Precisely at this point, midway in his career as a poet, Neruda comes to assume a new pose, spokesman for the continent, as he begins to work on his most ambitious project, the general song of America, *Canto general*. The poems of *Tercera residencia* close one cycle and clear the way for another.

Neruda in the Far East at the time he was writing the first *Residencia en la tierra,* about 1930

At the time of the
publication of the
first volume of
*Residencia en la
tierra* (1933)

Neruda in Buenos Aires (dedi-
cated to Héctor Eandi, 1933)

Neruda as Senator ("Yo acuso")

Este es el primer original
directo del primer canto
de mi obra "Canto General"
con las primeras correcciones.
Lo escribí en las horas de per-
secución del traidor González
Videla, al amparo de la hospi-
talidad de muchos chilenos
entre ellos Sergio y Aída In-
maza a quienes y a la adorada
pequeña Aída le dedico estos ori-
ginales como recuerdo y agrade-
cimiento en estos días errantes.

Pablo
Neruda

parque forestal julio de
1948

Manuscript page of *Canto general*

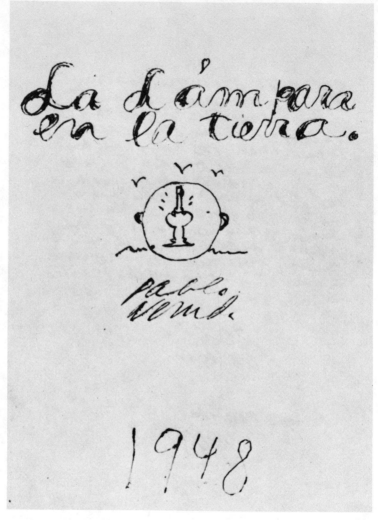

Manuscript page of "La lámpara en la tierra"

5. Epic Poetry
Canto general

No soy una campana de tan lejos,
ni un cristal enterrado tan profundo
que tú no puedas descifrar, soy sólo
pueblo, puerta escondida, pan oscuro,
y cuando me recibes, te recibes
a ti mismo, a ese huésped
tantas veces golpeado
y tantas veces
renacido.

1950

I am not a bell so distant, nor a crystal so deeply
buried that you can not decipher, I am only people,
hidden door, dark bread, and when you receive me,
you receive yourself, this guest beaten down so many
times and so many times reborn.

Canto general, the general song of America, presenting in
some five hundred pages and almost twenty thousand verses
the theme of man's struggle for justice in the New World,
caused a sensation when it appeared in 1950. Banned in Chile
for political reasons, and published in a limited printing in
Mexico by Ediciones Océano, it repeated on a much larger
scale the phenomenon of *Veinte poemas de amor y una canción
desesperada.* It was another succès de scandale. The mix of
praise and vituperation created curiosity, a curiosity which
was promptly satisfied in Mexico by a mass edition of some
five thousand copies—an extraordinary printing for a book of
poetry—and in Neruda's homeland by several clandestine edi-
tions prepared and distributed by the Chilean Communist
Party.

Today few would question the importance of this book in
the overall context of Neruda's œuvre. Yet, fewer still would be

in agreement concerning which of its poems are the most representative or significant. This paradoxical situation derives from the fact that critics split into two camps over the contents of this text: those who opposed Neruda's militant politics and those who shared them. For each of these views there arose two Nerudas, one good, one bad. Depending on the critic's political persuasion, the early poetry was either decadent or artistic, the later poetry ennobling or propagandistic. There was no middle ground; both sides forgot that there is an art even to propaganda, especially if it is to be effective. And *Canto general,* like *Tercera residencia,* was effective in that it both persuaded and provoked.

In this context the circumstances of its original publication are especially meaningful. The publishing centers of the Hispanic world are now Spain, Mexico, and Argentina. In 1950 the situation was much the same. However, Argentina under Perón and Spain under Franco did not offer an appropriate forum from which to launch a revisionist approach to the history of the Americas. Nor did Chile under Gabriel González Videla (who after being elected President with the support of the left in 1946 promptly initiated a Communist witch-hunt). Furthermore, the manuscript was inordinately long and costly to put into print. A subscription edition was the answer. As a consequence, and for reasons of expediency, *Canto general,* Neruda's most revolutionary work, was first published in Mexico City in a deluxe edition for bibliophiles, limited to five hundred copies, enriched with end-plates by Diego Rivera and David Alfaro Siqueiros. Sold by subscription, this work by a militant Communist—Neruda had joined the Party in 1945— made its debut as an elegant consumer product of the very bourgeois culture it so explicitly condemned. A contradition of capitalism, some would say, for the book's implied audience was not the subscribing elite but the man of the street. In fact, a mass edition soon appeared, a somewhat reduced facsimile of the original. The device of the subscription was really a means of subventing the printing costs. Within two years there was a second printing in Mexico of an additional five thousand copies; and in 1955, with the fall of Perón, the text was incorporated in the popular paperback series (Biblioteca clásica y contemporánea) of Argentina's Losada. It has been reprinted countless times since.

The controversy surrounding *Canto general* is best understood in the intellectual and political ambiance of 1950: the Cold War and its impact on the so-called "underdeveloped" countries. In this context the book was both timely and intriguing, presenting, as it did, the history of man in the New World as an epic saga of the underdog. Multiple narrators and a variety of literary styles ranging from the intensely lyrical to the stagily dramatic give this retelling an almost cinematic quality. Its immediate success, however, also owes something to coincidence. Its original publication in Mexico, while perhaps expedient, was also fortuitous, for it coincided there with *El laberinto de la soledad,* Octavio Paz's brilliant and influential essay reinterpreting Mexican history in a universal context.

Paz's book is a meditation on Mexico; Neruda's a mythification of America. Both are chronicles of self-discovery leading to a deeper awareness of cultural identification—what contemporary students of society call the "search for identity," a phenomenon common and peculiar to all the nations of the Americas. Former colonies administered as territorial extensions of Europe (New England, Nueva España, and so on), their political independence in the nineteenth century did not bring with it cultural independence. The language and culture of the Old World could not be extirpated with a simple Declaration of Independence; hence, the problem of identity. Paz and Neruda bring to this hoary problem a fresh perspective. They view their countries for the first time not merely as New World variants of the Greco-Roman past but as present-day sociopolitical realities. In this way they discover not what sets them apart as Chilean or Mexican, but what they and their people, midway through the twentieth century, ultimately share with other peoples of the hemisphere: cultural, political, and economic dependency. Thus, in 1950, and in *Canto general* and *El laberinto de la soledad* a kind of third-world consciousness was first voiced. This is the complementary quality that made both books so important in the Mexico of 1950. Neruda is again in the right place at the right time. The Mexican intellectuals of Paz's generation did for Neruda in Latin America what García Lorca and his friends had earlier done in Spain: they apotheosized him and treated his latest work as somehow prophetic.

While the similarities between *Canto general* and *El laberinto de la soledad* are important, there are also significant differences. Paz operates on the conviction that Mexico has finally come of age because of its Revolution; Neruda is more cautious on this point, showing that revolution is an ongoing process all over the continent and that it is necessary to carry it to completion. This is the purpose of *Canto general*: to convert the reader to the cause, to show him that solidarity of the oppressed is necessary to overcome the oppressor. To do this in a convincing way Neruda made use of literature's most venerable vehicle of propaganda, the epic, modernizing it through a complex system of dramatized narrators, creating in the process an almost cinematic narrative flow. The result was an engaging demythification of the clichés of textbook national histories with their panoply of exemplary bourgeois heroes. In their place he substituted a new, general history of the Americas, ecumenically mythifying an entire continent's struggle for social justice and political decency. The heroes of this epic adventure are ordinary men, collectively, the people.

The text is lengthy and has a complex breakdown: some five hundred pages, twenty thousand verses, three hundred and twenty poems all organized into fifteen major divisions, or cantos, these latter functioning much like chapters in a novel. The overall progression is chronological, moving from a pre-Columbian beginning to the present, the actual moment of composition. The initial poem, "Amor América" (Love for America), establishes the *illo tempore* of myth, that remote, almost forgotten moment when time was still and the world was new:

> Antes de la peluca y la casaca
> fueron los ríos, ríos arteriales:
> fueron las cordilleras, en cuya onda raída
> el cóndor o la nieve parecían inmóviles:
> fue la humedad y la espesura, el trueno
> sin nombre todavía, las pampas planetarias.
>
> El hombre tierra fue, vasija, párpado
> del barro trémulo, forma de la arcilla,
> fue cántaro caribe, piedra chibcha,
> copa imperial o sílice araucana.
> Tierno y sangriento fue, pero en la empuñadura
> de su arma de cristal humedecido,
> las iniciales de la tierra estaban
> escritas
>   Nadie pudo
> recordarlas después: el viento
> las olvidó, el idioma del agua
> fue enterrado, las claves se perdieron
> o se inundaron de silencio o sangre.
>
> No se perdió la vida, hermanos pastorales.
> Pero como una rosa salvaje
> cayó una gota roja en la espesura,
> y se apagó una lámpara de la tierra.
>
> Yo estoy aquí para contar la historia . . .*
>   (I, i, "Amor América")

Before the powdered wig and the cassock were the rivers, arterial rivers: there were mountains, in whose warm ripple the condor or the snow seemed immobile: there was humidity and density, the thunder was still unnamed, the plains planetary.   Man was earth, clay-pot eyelid of quivering mud, form of clay, he

---

* References to *Canto general* are indicated by the number of the canto and of the poem, and, when appropriate, the title.

was carribean water-vessel, chibcha stone, imperial cup or araucanian silex. Tender and bloody he was, but in the hilt of his weapon of wet crystal, the initials of the earth were written. No one could remember them afterwards: the wind forgot them, the language of water was buried, the keys were lost or inundated with silence or blood.   Life was not lost, pastoral brothers. But like a wild rose a red drop fell in the density, and one of the earth's lights was extinguished.   I am here to tell the story . . .

An extraordinary aura of vagueness and mystery is here evoked with a few relatively simple devices: suppression of the definite article in the second strophe, and the repeated use of the conjunction "o" (or) throughout the poem. In contrast, fifteen cantos later, in "Aquí termino" (I Finish Here), this same storyteller, Pablo Neruda himself, concludes on a somewhat different note, precise and matter-of-fact:

> Así termina este libro, aquí dejo
> mi *Canto general* escrito
> en la persecución, cantando bajo
> las alas clandestinas de mi patria.
> Hoy 5 de febrero, en este año
> de 1949, en Chile, en "Godomar
> de Chena," algunos meses antes
> de los cuarenta y cinco años de mi edad.
>
> (XV, xxviii, "Aquí termino")

Thus ends this book, here I leave my *Canto general* written under persecution, singing beneath the clandestine wings of my country. Today February 5, in this year 1949, in Chile, in "Godomar de Chena," several months before the forty-fifth year of my life.

Within this basic developmental scheme—the temporal passage from then to now—there is yet another major organizing principle, the internal thematic unity of each of the chapterlike cantos:

Each canto is itself internally organized on a chronological basis, proceeding from the genetic moment of the theme to its latest manifestation. The parade of heroes in Canto IV, for example, begins with Mexico's Cuauhtémoc (1520) and ends with Brazil's Prestes (1949). The array of tyrants that follows in "La arena traicionada" is similarly arranged in the order of time, moving from Doctor Francia, America's first dictator after independence from Spain, to González Videla, the latest (at the poem's writing). The pattern is the same in the other cantos. Certain cantos when taken together constitute a unit; the complete historical cycle comprised by the first five is obvious: Genesis to González Videla. The second five also reveal a developmental pattern, though somewhat more restricted in space and time; its chronological progression is contained in the contemporary period, largely within the Chilean experience. "América, no invoco tu nombre en vano" situates Chile in the concrete context of the continental situation circa 1940; Canto X is a Cid-like chronicle of the poet's contact with the Chilean people as a fugitive from González Videla's dragnet. The remaining group of five cantos (XI-XV) deals almost exclusively with Neruda's day-to-day experiences with his people since 1946, the year of his election to the Chilean Senate on the Communist Party ticket.

Thus, *Canto general* moves from the most remote moment of time to the most actual, from the most general historical event to the most particular and personal, from the poet as seer to the poet as comrade. In this way, the reader, as the poem progresses, is drawn closer to the principal narrative voice, who, beginning the poem in an authoritative biblical tone of prophecy, ends it in an intimate conversational style. Accordingly, each major section of the poem deepens the audience's understanding of a particular sociopolitical theme situated in its developing historical context. The systematically accumulative progression of the text is designed to move us from wonder to sympathy, from awe to pity. The purpose is to produce a kind of modern-day catharsis, a politicization of the reader, a conversion to the common cause of liberty and justice for all.

An overview of the genesis of the work permits us to appreciate the developing importance of the project as the author evolved ethically and aesthetically. In the winter of 1938, not long after having published "España en el corazón," Neruda founded a new literary journal in Santiago, the *Aurora de Chile*. Its first issue contains an ode to the river Mapocho, the desert stream whose headwaters are in the Andes and on whose muddy banks Santiago de Chile was originally settled by the Spaniards. The poem's style and content reflect the conversion effected in Spain under the twin influences of Quevedo and the Civil War:

> Río, por qué conduces
> agua fría y secreta,
> agua que el alba dura de las piedras

guardó en su catedral inaccesible,
hasta los pies heridos de mi pueblo?
Vuelve, vuelve a tu copa de nieve, río amargo,
vuelve, vuelve a tu copa de espaciosas escarchas,
sumerge tu plateada raíz en tu secreto origen
o despéñate y rómpete en otro mar sin lágrimas!
Río Mapocho cuando la noche llega
y como negra estatua echada
duerme bajo tus puentes con un racimo negro
de cabezas golpeadas por el frío y el hambre
como por dos immensas águilas, oh río,
oh duro río parido por la nieve,
por qué no te levantas como inmenso fantasma
o como nueva cruz de estrellas para los olvidados?

. . . que una gota de tu espuma negra
salte del légamo a la flor del fuego
y precipite la semilla del hombre!

River, why do you carry cold and secret water, water that the hard dawn of stone kept in its inaccessible cathedral, right to the wounded feet of my people? Go back, go back to your cupful of snow, bitter river, go back, go back to your cupful of spatious frosts, submerge your silvery root in your secret origins or fling yourself down and let yourself loose in another sea of tears! River Mapocho when night arrives and like a black statue stretched-out it sleeps beneath your bridges with a black bunch of heads bruised by cold and hunger as though by two immense eagles, oh river oh hard river born of snow, why don't you rise up like an immense ghost or like a new cross of stars for the forgotten people?   . . . would that one drop of your black foam leap from the silt to the flower of fire and precipitate the seed of man!

The poet's new humanism, the need for social justice, and the Quevedian notion that death leads to life are evident in this 1938 composition, Neruda's first concerned with a social theme in an American context. But this "Oda de invierno al río Mapocho" (Winter Ode to the River Mapocho) was not collected in *Tercera residencia* along with the other political poetry of the period 1935–1945. Actually, it was the seed poem of a separate undertaking, a "Canto general de Chile," later to become *Canto general*. While in Mexico, in 1940, the poet spoke to Maurice Halperin of *Books Abroad* about a new project he was then working on, "a long epic poem on his native land." According to Neruda:

> It will have descriptive and lyric elements as well, and will attempt to reveal the deep process of historic transformation through which Chile has passed. I want to counter-balance the effect of the great poetry of the classics, such as Ercilla and Pedro de Oña. But I feel very humble in this task. To write for the people is too great an ambition.*

His "Canto para Bolívar," the 1941 poem included in *Tercera residencia* shares this populist orientation and also transcends the Chilean context here circumscribed by the author. And it is in this wider, continental direction that Neruda's epic was ultimately to develop, becoming a general song not only of Chile but also of America. While in Mexico he continued to work on the project and published several other compositions later integrated into *Canto general*.† The most important of these for an overview of the generative development of the project is perhaps "América, no invoco tu nombre en vano." Written in 1943, as Neruda was preparing to leave Mexico, it is unique in its solid portrayal of the poet in his newly assumed role as miltant spokesman for America, as the outspoken conscience of the entire continent:

---

* "Pablo Neruda in Mexico," *Books Abroad*, 15:168 (Spring 1941).

† "Oratorio menor en la muerte de Silvestre Revueltas," *El Nacional* (Mexico), October 7, 1940; "Tocopilla," "Quiero volver al sur," *Letras de México*, 3:4 (April 15, 1941); "El corazón magallánico," *Cuadernos Americanos* (March–April 1942); "Melancolía cerca de Orizaba," *Cuadernos Americanos* (March–April 1943); "América, no invoco tu nombre en vano," *América*, no. 19 (July 1943).

América, no invoco tu nombre en vano.
Cuando sujeto al corazón la espada,
cuando aguanto en el alma la gotera,
cuando por las ventanas
un nuevo día tuyo me penetra,
soy y estoy en la luz que me produce,
vivo en la sombra que me determina,
duermo y despierto en tu esencial aurora:
dulce como las uvas, y terrible,
conductor del azúcar y el castigo,
empapado en esperma de tu especie,
amamantado en sangre de tu herencia.

(VI, xviii)

America, I do not take your name in vain. When I put my heart
to the sword, when I endure in my soul your draining away,
when through the windows your new day penetrates me, I exist
and I am present in the light which produces me, I live in the
shadow that outlines me, I sleep and I awake in your essential
aurora: sweet as grapes, and terrible, conduit of sugar and
punishment, soaked in sperm of your species, nursed on blood
of your inheritance.

This selfsame oracular tone will come to identify the principal
narrative voice throughout *Canto general* as the voice of Pablo
Neruda, *poeta mayor*. Such a presumptive narrative posture
was exactly what was needed to "counterbalance" the weight
of tradition Neruda had mentioned to Halperin. In this way,
like a biblical prophet, he was to speak to his people.

It is significant that it was also in 1943, on Neruda's re-
turn trip to Chile, that he visited Peru and made the trek to
Macchu Picchu, the long-lost city of the Incas perched on a
seven-thousand-foot mountaintop. Out of this came, "Alturas
de Macchu Picchu," a mystic poem in twelve parts, not un-
like the stations of the cross, chronicling the poet's peregrina-
tion and presenting in religious terms his personal attainment
of a continental vision. First published in 1946, and later in-
corporated as the second canto of *Canto general*, this is the

text that in the larger literary context of the complete work, authenticates the poet's voice and authorizes him to speak out for the hemisphere. What was merely assumed in "América, no invoco tu nombre en vano" is symbolically convoked before the ruins of the dead city at the poem's conclusion:

> Yo vengo a hablar por vuestra boca muerta.
> A través de la tierra juntad todos
> los silenciosos labios derramados
> y desde el fondo habladme toda esta larga noche,
> como si yo estuviera con vosotros anclado,
> contadme todo, cadena a cadena,
> eslabón a eslabón, y paso a paso,
> afilad los cuchillos que guardasteis,
> ponedlos en mi pecho y en mi mano,
> como un río de rayos amarillos,
> como un río de tigres enterrados,
> y dejadme llorar, horas, días, años,
> edades ciegas, siglos estelares.
>
> Dadme el silencio, el agua, la esperanza.
>
> Dadme la lucha, el hierro, los volcanes.
>
> Apegadme los cuerpos como imanes.
>
> Acudid a mis venas y a mi boca.
>
> Hablad por mis palabras y mi sangre.
>
> (II, xii)

I come to speak through your dead mouth. From across the earth bring together all the silent scattered lips and from the depths speak to me through this long night, as though I were anchored down with you, tell me everything, chain by chain, link by link, and step by step, sharpen the knives you put away, put them in my chest and in my hand, like a river of yellow rays, like a river of buried tigers, and let me weep, hours, days, years, blind ages, light-centuries.   Give me silence, water, hope.   Give me the struggle, the iron, the volcanoes.   Stick bodies on me like magnets.   Come to my veins and my mouth.   Speak through my words and my blood.

Thus, by 1946 Neruda had significantly expanded the thematic scope of his original project and developed an appropriate narrative vehicle for its delivery. But, owing to the political exigencies of the time, the poem itself would not be completed until 1949, and then only under the most trying of conditions.

In 1945 Neruda joined the Chilean Communist Party. It was a peculiar moment in Chile and the world, one in which the same issue of *El Siglo* (the official organ of the Party in Chile) that publishes his entrance speech could also carry a front-page photo of Churchill, Truman, and Stalin as "tres campeones de la paz" (three champions of peace).* This moment was short-lived, however, for the Cold War was already getting under way. No sooner was the poet elected Senator from Tarapacá, in 1946, than the Communist Party was outlawed, and Neruda became a fugitive. It was then, hiding from the police, that he finally completed the book. Canto X, "El fugitivo," begins by giving an epic sweep to the poet's flight, stressing at the same time his vital link with his people:

> Por la alta noche, por la vida entera,
> de lágrima a papel, de ropa en ropa,
> anduve en estos días abrumados.
> Fui el fugitivo de la policía:
> y en la hora de cristal, en la espesura
> de estrellas solitarias,
> crucé ciudades, bosques,
> chacarerías, puertos,
> de la puerta de un ser humano a otro,
> de la mano de un ser a otro ser, a otro ser.
>
> (X, i)

Through the middle of the night, through all of life, from tear to paper, from rag to rag, I wandered in these turbulent days. I was a fugitive from the police: and in the hour of crystal, in

* "Palabras de Pablo Neruda al ingresar al Partido Comunista de Chile," *El Siglo* (Santiago), July 9, 1945.

> the thickness of solitary stars, I crossed cities, forests, farms, ports, from the door of one human being to another from the hand of one to another, to another.

Curiously enough, these unfortunate circumstances, poetized mostly in the latter portions of *Canto general,* actually enhanced the poem's total significance, rendering it more persuasive. The documentary quality, so basic to epic discourse, was strengthened; the absolute past and the lived present were, in a sense, compressed so as to occupy the same plane of narration. The present experienced as past in this way authenticated the revisioned past.

Canto general was completed on February 5, 1949, and on February 24 Pablo Neruda clandestinely crossed the Andes into the Argentina of Perón, carrying with him the manuscript (disguised as *Risas y lágrimas* by one Benigno Espinoza). Not long afterward he surfaced in Paris, his arrival there coinciding with a World Peace Congress. Picasso was waiting, as Neruda himself recorded:

> In Paris I destroyed my false documents and I recovered my true identity. Picasso was waiting for me. Only a month before he had made the first public speech of his life and he was as happy as a child. The speech was about my disappearance. And now with brotherly concern, the great genius, minotaur of painting, monster of modern nature, was occupying himself with the most minute details of my situation, speaking with the authorities, telephoning everybody . . . During these days a Peace Congress was being celebrated in Paris. I showed up there at the last moment to read some of my poems. Everyone applauded me and embraced me. Many had thought me dead.*

Very much alive, Neruda was lionized in Paris, a circumstance, given the cultural dependency of the New World, that ironically lent further authority to his newly adopted oracular

---

* "Memorias," *O Cruzeiro Internacional,* May 16, 1962, p. 37.

role as continental spokesman. From France he went on to Mexico, to yet another Peace Congress where he arranged the publication of *Canto general.*

Through this overview we can see that the idea for a narrative poem reinterpreting the historical past originated in a moment of crisis, shortly after the poet's political consciousness was raised in Spain. It was developed in Chile and in Mexico during and after the Second World War, at a time when the Western Hemisphere nations seemed to hold out a last hope for justice and democracy. *Canto general* is thus a peculiarly American poem, infused with optimism. The thesis was simple: the New World triumphs over the Old, life over death. As Europe looks existentially inward, melancholically contemplating its own death throes, America is on the threshold of a new life. It is this messianic optimism that makes Neruda's 1950 poem so smugly American, so noxiously anti-European. In one major section, "La arena traicionada," the Europeanizing poets of the past are called to task as traitors to the cause:

> Qué hicisteis vosotros gidistas,
> intelectualistas, rilkistas,
> misterizantes, falsos brujos
> existenciales, amapolas
> surrealistas encendidas
> en una tumba, europeizados
> cadáveres de la moda,
> pálidas lombrices del queso
> capitalista, qué hicisteis
> ante el reinado de la angustia,
> frente a este oscuro ser humano,
> a esta pateada compustura,
> a esta cabeza sumergida
> en el estiércol, a esta esencia
> de ásperas vidas pisoteadas?
>
> No hicisteis nada sino la fuga . . .
>   (V, ii, "Los poetas celestes," The Celestial Poets)

What did you Gidists do, intellectualists, Rilkists, mysterizers, fake existential shamans, surrealist poppies burning in a tomb, Europeanized cadavers a la mode, pallid worms of the capitalist cheese, what did you do at the kingdom of anguish, faced with this obscure human being, with this kicked-out composure, with this head submerged in dung, with this essence of harsh lives trampled over? You did nothing but flee . . .

The virulent, acerbic tone is not unlike that of Quevedo. But, wasn't Neruda's earliest *Residencia* poetry similarly existential in its concerns? Indeed it was, and perhaps for this very reason *Canto general* contains several treatments of what can now be recognized as a relatively constant subtheme in Neruda's mature work, the topic of his "conversion," his cyclic renewal in literature. "Los ríos del canto" contains an intimate poem, "Carta a Miguel Otero Silva, en Caracas, 1948" (Letter to Miguel Otero Silva, in Caracas, 1948) which registers the poet's awareness of his transformation and the effect it has on his readers:

Cuando yo escribía versos de amor, que me brotaban
por todas partes, y me moría de tristeza,
errante, abandonado, royendo el alfabeto,
me decían: "Qué grande eres, oh Teócrito!"
Yo no soy Teócrito: tomé a la vida,
me puse frente a ella, la besé hasta vencerla,
y luego me fui por los callejones de las minas
a ver cómo vivían otros hombres.
Y cuando salí con las manos teñidas de basura y dolores,
las levanté mostrándolas en las cuerdas de oro,
y dije: "Yo no comparto el crimen."
Tosieron, se disgustaron mucho, me quitaron el saludo,
me dejaron de llamar Teócrito, y terminaron
por insultarme y mandar toda la policía a encarcelarme,
por que no seguía preocupado exclusivamente de asuntos
   metafísicos.

(XII, i)

When I wrote verses of love, that burst from me everywhere, and I was dying of sadness, wandering, abandoned, gnawing on the alphabet, they used to say to me: "How great you are Theocritus!" I am not Theocritus: I took life, I faced up to it, I kissed it until I conquered it, and then I went through the passages of the mines to see how other men lived. And when I came out with my hands stained with refuse and pain, I lifted them up showing them to the strands of gold, and I said: "I do not share in the crime." People coughed, they were very upset, they refused to greet me, they stopped calling me Theocritus, and they ended up by insulting me and by calling all the police to jail me, because I did not continue to be concerned exclusively with metaphysical things.

What is here so airily recounted in the guise of a letter from the fugitive poet was earlier dealt with in a more public fashion in "Alturas de Macchu Picchu," the 1946 poem which became Canto II in Neruda's epic and served as a kind of touchstone for the sincerity of the poet's conversion and commitment. We have seen how in the last of this canto's twelve parts, the speaker, transformed before the ruins of Macchu Picchu, calls out to the continent's dead, asking them to speak through him. The poet's transformation itself though is actually presented in the sixth part, and in decidedly mystic terms. The first five review Neruda's previous literary stages, his failed attempts to attain a truly meaningful literary expression which could be ethically and aesthetically harmonious. They begin with a condemning reference to the muddled futility of his crepuscular poetry:

Del aire al aire, como una red vacía,
iba yo entre las calles y la atmósfera, llegando y despidiendo . . .

From air to air, like an empty net, I would go through the streets and the atmosphere, arriving and saying goodbye . . .

This is the road of trials, the dark night of the soul which preludes change. And it is in the sixth section, reproduced below in its entirety, that the poet's transformation is presented in mystic terms patterned after Fray Luis de León's "Noche serena." The Spanish mystic's "morada de grandeza" (place of greatness) is here Macchu Picchu:

> Entonces en la escala de la tierra he subido
> entre la atroz maraña de las selvas perdidas
> hasta ti, Macchu Picchu.
> Alta ciudad de piedras escalares,
> (5) por fin morada del que lo terrestre
> no escondió en las dormidas vestiduras.
> En ti, como dos líneas paralelas,
> la cuna del relámpago y del hombre
> se mecían en un viento de espinas.
>
> (10) Madre de piedra, espuma de los cóndores.
>
> Alto arrecife de la aurora humana.
>
> Pala perdida en la primera arena.
>
> Esta fue la morada, éste es el sitio:
> aquí los anchos granos del maíz ascendieron
> (15) y bajaron de nuevo como granizo rojo.
>
> Aquí la hebra dorada salió de la vicuña
> a vestir los amores, los túmulos, las madres,
> el rey, las oraciones, los guerreros.
>
> Aquí los pies del hombre descansaron de noche
> (20) junto a los pies del águila en las altas guaridas
> carniceras, y en la aurora
> pisaron con los pies del trueno la niebla enrarecida
> y tocaron las tierras y las piedras
> hasta reconocerlas en la noche o la muerte.
>
> (25) Miro las vestiduras y las manos,
> el vestigio del agua en la oquedad sonora,
> la pared suavizada por el tacto de un rostro
> que miró con mis ojos las lámparas terrestres,
> que aceitó con mis manos las desaparecidas
> (30) maderas: porque todo, ropaje, piel, vasijas,
> palabras, vino, panes,
> se fue, cayó a la tierra.

Y el aire entró con dedos
de azahar sobre todos los dormidos:
(35) mil años de aire, meses, semanas de aire,
de viento azul, de cordillera férrea,
que fueron como suaves huracanes de pasos
lustrando el solitario recinto de la piedra.

(II, vi)

Then up the ladder of the earth I climbed through the heavy
tangle of lost jungles unto you, Macchu Picchu. High city of
laddered stones, finally a resting place from which the terrestrial
did not hide in its weary garments. In you, as two parallel lines,
the cradle of lightning and of man rocked in a wind of
thorns.   Mother of stone, sperm of condors.   High reef
of human dawn. Spade buried in primordial sand.   This was
the resting place, this is the site: here the fat grains of corn
grew up and fell down again in a red hail.   Here the golden
thread came from the vicuña to clothe loves, tombs, mothers,
the king, prayers, warriors.   Here men's feet rested at night
next to the feet of eagles, in the high carnivorous haunts, and
at dawn they stomped with feet of thunder the rarified mists,
and they touched the dirt and the stones until finding in them
night or death.   I look at clothes and hands, the remains
of water in the sonorous cavity, the wall smoothed by the touch
of a face that looked with my eyes on earth's lights, that oiled
with my hands the vanished wood: because everything, clothes,
skin, pots, words, wine, bread, is gone, fallen to earth.   And
the air came in with fingers of blossoms over all the sleeping
ones: a thousand years of air, months, weeks of air, of blue wind,
of iron mountains, that went on like soft hurricanes of foot-
steps, shining the solitary site of stone.

The soul of the poet is united not with nature or with God,
as in traditional mystic poetry, but with the continent and
its past history. The strophic divisions correspond to discrete
stages of the symbolic communion which transforms the poet,
giving him a continental mission. The first strophe, of
nine verses, is meditative and evokes Macchu Picchu as the

"morada," the true residence, the final stopping place in Neruda's personal quest for life's meaning. The hallowed mood is intensified in verses 10–12, whose three formulaic invocations present a kind of litany to stone, making of the mountain city of the Incas a very sacred place, the godhead of history. Then, in a series of three strophes (verses 13–24), the transforming vision occurs, permitting the poet to witness the past in the present. Finally able to see what before he had not even dared to imagine, he is transformed from contemplator of the remote past to its voiced presence. In the penultimate strophe the speaker's vision is fused with that of the former inhabitants of the dead city. He sees with their eyes, they with his. This transferral is achieved by using the same verb ("mirar," to look) in two distinct forms (different person, different tense, same spelling), thus linguistically fusing the past and the present, the seer and the seen. The speaker is finally one with the past, its present-day embodiment:

> *Miro* las vestiduras y las manos,
> el vestigio del agua en la oquedad sonora,
> la pared suavizada por el tacto de un rostro
> que *miró con mis ojos* las lámparas terrestres.

In this way, Neruda both mythified his conversion and authenticated the poem's principal narrative voice; the mystic communion with the past poetized in "Alturas de Macchu Picchu" authorizes the poet to speak with a voice of biblical authority for all the people of the Americas. Its people are his people. He is in them.

This oracular pose also permitted the author to speak out through a host of other distinct narrative voices in the remaining cantos, turning his *Canto general* into a truly general song, a choral epic. For example, as the history unfolds and the epic conflict begins, Pedro de Valdivia, the sixteenth-century conquistador, is taken captive by the fierce Araucanian Indians; the narrative voice then is not that of the poet Pablo Neruda but Lautaro, the champion of his people's independence. His narrative and its shocking imagery are designed to confound the reader, forcing a revision of certain received attitudes regarding the heroic Spanish conquest:

> Llevamos a Valdivia bajo el árbol . . .
> Luego golpeamos el rostro enemigo.
> Luego cortamos el valiente cuello.
> ` Qué hermosa fue la sangre del verdugo
> que repartimos como una granada,
> mientras ardía viva todavía.
> Luego, en el pecho entramos una lanza
> y el corazón alado como un ave
> entregamos al árbol araucano.
> Subió un rumor de sangre hasta su copa.
>
> Entonces, de la tierra
> hecha de nuestros cuerpos, nació el canto
> de la guerra, del sol, de las cosechas,
> hacia la magnitud de los volcanes.
> Entonces repartimos el corazón sangrante.
> Yo hundí los dientes en aquella corola
> cumpliendo el rito de la tierra:
> "Dame tu frío, extranjero malvado.
> "Dame tu valor de gran tigre.
> "Dame en tu sangre tu cólera . . ."
>   (IV, xii, "El corazón de Pedro de Valdivia," The
>   Heart of Pedro de Valdivia)

We put Valdivia under the tree . . .   Then we beat on the enemy's face.   Next we cut off his valiant head.   How lovely was the scourge's blood that we passed around like a pomegranate, while it was still burning with life. Next, in his chest we stuck a spear and his heart winged like a bird we gave to the Araucanian tree. A murmur of blood rushed up to its crown.   Then, from the earth made of our bodies, rose up a song of war, of the sun, of crops, toward the magnitude of the volcanoes. Then we passed around his bloody heart. I sunk

my teeth in that corolla carrying out the rites of the land:
"Give me your coldness, evil foreigner. Give me your courage
of a great tiger. Give me in your blood your anger . . ."

This is truly a revisionist view of history, for its factual point
of departure is the established tradition, the reality most fa-
miliar to the reader. A simple shift in the narrative point of
view is all that is needed to make the renegade Lautaro into
a liberator and the noble Valdivia a villain. Having the pro-
tagonist relate the story in this way makes for a portrayal
which is at once both dramatic and objective. As a conse-
quence, history is not arbitrarily reinterpreted, it is directly
represented, re-created. The audience, shocked by the macabre
imagery of the bloodthirsty narrator, is thrust into a new role;
it is forced to reinterpret what it already knows, to judge the
past from another perspective.

Bertold Brecht used alienation as a device to jolt the audi-
ence into into a new level of consciousness. What he did for
epic theater Neruda does for epic poetry with very much the
same technique: multiple protagonists and sudden shifts in
narrative voice. The procedure, used systematically throughout
the poem, is especially effective in those portions dealing with
the contemporary period, the period for which the reader al-
ready has a formed opinion. In Canto VIII, "La tierra se llama
Juan," the historic moment is now. Multiple narrators make the
revisionist view seem accordingly to be less the opinion of one
person than the collective expression of the entire continent.
A kind of alienation is achieved as Pablo Neruda inserts him-
self in the narrative system as spectator, illustrating the fact
that our role, like his, is first to witness and then to judge. A
score of contemporaries, laborers all, parade before us re-
counting life's tragedy, its poverty, exploitation, and injustice.
They are the living dead, victims of the present economic
system, and as each one speaks out, we listen along with
Neruda:

Usted es Neruda? Pase, camarada.
Sí, de la Casa del Yodo, ya no quedan
otros viviendo. Yo me aguanto.
Sé que ya no estoy vivo, que me espera
la tierra de la pampa. Son cuatro horas
al día, en la Casa del Yodo.
Viene por unos tubos, sale como una masa,
como una goma cárdena. La entramos
de batea en batea, la envolvemos
como criatura. Mientras tanto,
el ácido nos roe, nos socava,
entrando por los ojos y la boca,
por la piel, por las uñas.
De la Casa del Yodo no se sale
cantando, compañero . . .
    (VIII, xi, "Juan Figueroa, Casa del Yodo 'María Elena,'
    Antofagasta," Juan Figueroa, Iodine Factory "Maria
                 Elena," Antofagasta)

You are Neruda? Go ahead, comrade. Yes, from the Iodine
Factory, now there remain no others living. I endure. I know
that I am not alive anymore, that the dirt of the plains, awaits
me. It is four hours a day, in the Iodine Factory. It comes in
through some tubes, it goes out like a blob, like a livid paste.
We make it go from one tub to another, we wrap it up like a
child. Meanwhile, the acid eats into us, bores into us, getting
in through our eyes and mouth, through our skin, through our
nails. From the Iodine Factory you don't leave singing,
friend . . .

Others step forward to relate their tales of misfortune with
individually characteristic rhythms and syntax. A miner from
Bolivia speaks with the humble cadence and awkward word
order of the partially acculturated Indian of the highlands:

Sí señor, José Cruz Achachalla,
de la Sierra de Granito, al sur de Oruro.
Pues allí debe vivir aún

mi madre Rosalía:
a unos señores trabaja,
lavándoles, pues, la ropa.
Hambre pasábamos, capitán,
y con una varilla golpeaban
a mi madre todos los días.
Por eso me hice minero . . .
>(VIII, ix, "Jose Cruz Achachalla, minero, Bolivia," José
>Cruz Achachalla, miner, Bolivia)

Yes sir, José Cruz Achachalla, from the Sierra de Granito, south of Oruro. Well there she ought to be living still my mother Rosalía: for some people she works, washing for them, well, their clothes. We were very hungry, captain, and with a rod they would beat my mother every day. That's why I became a miner . . .

A worker's wife, politicized by the repressive regime, speaks out somewhat more declaratively:

Arreglé la comida a mis chiquillos y salí.
Quise entrar a Lota a ver a mi marido.
Como se sabe, mandan la policía
y nadie puede entrar sin su permiso.
Les cayó mal mi cara. Eran las órdenes
de González Videla, antes de entrar
a decir sus discursos, para que nuestra gente
tenga miedo . . .
>(VIII, xiv, "Benilda Varela, Concepción, Ciudad
>Universitaria, Chile, 1949")

I fixed a meal for my kids and went out. I wanted to get into Lota to see my husband. As you know, the police are in command and no one can enter without their permission. They didn't like my face. There were orders from González Videla, before coming to make his speeches, so that our people would be afraid . . .

And so it continues. The common denominator is abuse and repression. All these cases read like a docket for the Last

Judgment and serve implicitly as an indictment of a system based on exploitation and fostering tyranny. These suffering people are presented in the poem as dramatized narrators, individuated representatives of a class, the working poor. They are not social misfits; they are the victims of an unjust and repressive socioeconomic system. Toward the end of the canto Neruda changes roles; passing from witness to judge, he voices the collective judgment of the people, his people:

> Y esto es cuanto quería deciros, camaradas:
> hacc falta el castigo.
> No puede ser este derrumbe humano,
> esta sangría de la patria amada,
> esta sangre que cae del corazón del pueblo
> cada minuto, esta muerte
> de cada hora.
> Yo me llamo como ellos, como los que murieron.
> Yo soy también Ramírez, Múñoz, Pérez, Fernández.
> Me llamo Alvárez, Núñez, Tapia, López, Contreras.
> Soy pariente de todos los que mueren, soy pueblo . . .
>   (VIII, xvi, "Castástrofe en Sewell," Catastrophe
>   at Sewell)

And this is all I wanted to tell you, comrades: punishment is necessary. This human downfall cannot be, this bleeding of the beloved country, this blood that falls from the heart of the people each minute, this death of every hour. I am named like them, like those who died. I am also Ramírez, Múñoz, Pérez, Fernández. I am named Alvárez, Núñez, Tapia, López, Contreras. I am a relative of all those who die, I am the people . . .

And finally, the reader too is included in the canto's referential system as the poet concludes invoking the contemporary dead to speak not only to him and through him, as at Macchu Picchu, but through us as well. Together, we are now to continue where they left off:

Compatriotas, hermanos muertos, de Sewell, muertos
de Chile, obreros, hermanos, camaradas,
hoy que estáis silenciosos, vamos a hablar nosotros.
Y que vuestro martirio nos ayude
a construir una patria severa
que sepa florecer y castigar.

(VIII, xvi)

Countrymen, dead brothers, of Sewell, dead of Chile, workers,
brothers, comrades, today you are silent, we are going to speak.
And may your martyrdom aid us in constructing a stern coun-
try that knows how to prosper and to punish.

The narrative "I" is varied here and throughout *Canto
general* to create the illusion of a collective perspective de-
signed consistently to involve the reader. The purpose is to
engage us not only aesthetically but also ideologically. The
epic has always been a form of artistic propaganda, but it tra-
ditionally functioned not as a text to be read but one to be
performed, as a kind of narrative spectacle, more theatrical
than literary. For this reason a prayerful intonation like the
conclusion to "Castástrofe en Sewell" may seem out of place
in a traditional epic poem, while it is extremely effective in
the literary context of *Canto general* where, as in Canto VIII,
it can operate as an epilogue, a closing textual aside addressed
obliquely to the reader and designed to round out the narrative
plan of the work, to stress once again its ideological thrust.

Thus far we have limited our attention to one kind of
literary procedure, by far the most salient of *Canto general,*
the special use of the narrative "I" wherein the speaker is
protagonist of the action he is describing. In a traditional epic
the narrator is a somewhat distant witness, a spectator of the
described events. Variety could be introduced and monotony
avoided only within the rather limited perspective of the nar-
rator's singular point of observation: hence the importance
of focus and detailed description to maintain audience inter-
est between the high points of the various episodes. Neruda

employs this time-honored procedure as well; in fact, the descriptive portions of his modern epic serve an additional purpose. For their artfulness alone they are constant reminders that *Canto general* is a poem, a literary construct (and not just a tract of propaganda in verse).

The epic belongs to the oral tradition of narrative poetry and once it passes onto the printed page, becoming in the process literature, it loses· much of the vitality derived from the performance aspect of live narration. It is then a narrative text to be read. The performance must take place in the mind of the reader. Straight narrative, therefore, runs the risk of lulling modern readers into the feeling that we are dealing with prose not poetry, with a fictive novel and not an historically factual epic poem. The difference is in the reading, the distinct attitudes we are conditioned to bring to poetry as opposed to prose. Neruda, sensitive to this literary problem since the time of the first *Residencia en la tierra* (which contained separate sections of prose and poetry), overcomes the special difficulty it poses in a long text by carefully alternating direct narrative action with lyric, descriptive, and even comic passages, creating thereby the kind of literary tension necessary for an appropriate reader response.

Returning briefly to the Lautaro section of Canto IV ("Los libertadores"), we can get an idea as to how this process works. The poems immediately preceeding Lautaro's dramatic first-person narration are highly stylized voice-over descriptions of distinct stages of the hero's life, from his birth to his people's revolt against Valdivia. Poem ix, dealing with the "Educación del cacique" (The Chief's Education), for example, is presented as a series of brief declarative enunciations. The succession of single-verse phrases and the exotic quality of the metaphoric imagery they contain gives a kind of otherworldly onrush to the chief's coming of age:

> Fue su primera edad sólo silencio.
> Su adolescencia fue dominio.

Su juventud fue un viento dirigido.
Se preparó como una larga lanza.
Acostumbró los pies en las cascadas.
Educó la cabeza en las espinas.
Ejecutó las pruebas del guanaco.
Vivió en las madrigueras de la nieve.
Acechó la comida de las águilas.
Arañó los secretos del peñasco.
Entretuvo los pétalos del fuego.
Se amamantó de primavera fría.
Se quemó en las gargantas infernales . . .

(IV, ix)

His early age was only silence. His adolescence was domination.
His youth was a directed wind. He prepared himself like a long
lance. He accustomed his feet in the cascades. He trained his
head in the thorns. He fulfilled the trials of the guanaco. He
lived in the burrows of snow. He stalked the food of eagles.
He scratched the secrets from the stone. He entertained the
petals of fire. He nursed himself in the cold Spring. He burned
himself in the infernal gullets . . .

This strange litany, which goes on for thirty-eight verses, con-
ditions the reader for the concluding statement: "Sólo entonces
fue digno de su pueblo" (Only then was he worthy of his peo-
ple). Lautaro, elevated in this way to a noble stature, is then
put into action. The style changes accordingly. In a subsequent
section, as he and his men stalk Valdivia, the strophic distribu-
tion of the verses and displaced margins are visual devices
Neruda uses to modulate the textual flow of words so as to
create a pace and tension not unlike that of a dramatized oral
delivery:

Se abrió paso en las húmedas marañas
del crepúsculo austral.
            Llegó Lautaro,
en un galope negro de caballos.

La fatiga y la muerte conducían
la tropa de Valdivia en el follaje.

Se acercaban las lanzas de Lautaro.

Entre los muertos y las hojas iba
como en un túnel Pedro de Valdivia.

En las tinieblas llegaba Lautaro . . .
(IV, xi, "Lautaro contra el Centauro, 1554," Lautaro
versus the Centaur, 1544)

A path was opened in the humid jungles of the Southern dawn.
Lautaro arrived in a black gallop of horses.   Fatigue and
death were guiding the troops of Valdivia in the foliage.   The
lances of Lautaro were getting closer.   Among the dead and
the leaves he fled as though in a tunnel, Pedro de Valdivia.   In
the darkness Lautaro was arriving . . .

As the story goes on, Pedro de Valdivia is captured; and for
the ensuing episode the narrative style changes once again,
the speaker becoming Lautaro ("Llevamos a Valdivia bajo el
árbol . . ." IV, xii), thus enhancing the overall dramatic effect.

The form and style of the indivdual poems making up *Canto
general* is continually varied by Neruda in a systematic effort
to engage the reader's aesthetic interest and keep him read-
ing the work as a poem and experiencing it as drama. In this
way the reader will accord to the text the special hermeneutic
attention conventionally reserved for these genres. Accord-
ingly, every composition's literary style is a direct and recog-
nizable function of its content. A most telling example of this
is found in a poem dealing with Francisco de Miranda (1750–
1816), the Venezuelan revolutionist and adventurer. As an
officer in the Spanish Army he fought against England in the
American Revolution. Later, in Europe he fought in the
French Revolution and was at one time a favorite of Catherine
the Great. After the outbreak of the Spanish American Revolu-
tion he returned to Venezuela and was Supreme Commander
there before surrendering to the Spanish in 1812. Denounced

by Bolívar, he eventually died in a dungeon in Cádiz, Spain, trusted by no one. Neruda evokes this strange figure in a run-on narrative style whose sequential confusion mirrors the muddled adventures of Miranda. A rather tight metrical regularity (mostly hendecasyllables) incongruously comes up against a total lack of punctuation, a textual device that modulates by its very absence:

> Si entráis a Europa tarde con sombrero
> de copa en el jardín condecorado
> por más de un Otoño junto al mármol
> de la fuente mientras caen hojas
> de oro harapiento en el Imperio
> si la puerta recorta una figura
> sobre la noche de San Petersburgo
> tiemblan los cascabeles del trineo
> y alguien en la soledad blanca alguien
> el mismo paso la misma pregunta
> si tú sales por la florida puerta
> de Europa un caballero sombra traje
> inteligencia signo cordón de oro
> Libertad Igualdad mira su frente
> entre la artillería que truena . . .
> (IV, xxiii, "Miranda muere en la niebla, 1816," Miranda
> Dies in the Fog, 1816)

If you enter Europe late with a top / hat in the garden adorned / by more than one Autumn next to the marble / of the fountain while fall leaves / of threadbare gold in the Empire / of the door outlines a figure / on the night of Saint Petersburg / the bells of the sleigh tinkle / and someone in the white solitude someone / the same step the same question / if you leave by the florid door / of Europe a gentleman shadow suit / intelligence sign golden cord / Liberty Equality look at his face, / among the artillery that rumbles . . .

A stylized disarticulation, more oneiric here than in any *Residencia* poem, presents directly—and objectively—this controversial figure, both hero and traitor to the cause of liberty. The reader must sort through the confusion of the composition, and consequently of Miranda's role in the struggle. Conversely, when coupled with free verse and a straightforward continuous discourse, the same suppression of punctuation in a section concerned with Abraham Lincoln creates another kind of lyric flow, an eerie serenity pregnant with an impending disorder (racial conflict):

> A veces el viento del Sur resbala
> sobre la sepultura de Lincoln trayendo
> voces y briznas de ciudades y árboles
> nada pasa en su tumba las letras no se mueven
> el mármol se suaviza con lentitud de siglos
> el viejo caballero ya no vive
> no existe el agujero de su antigua camisa
> se han mezclado las fibras de tiempo y polvo humano
> qué vida tan cumplida dice una temblorosa
> señora de Virginia una escuela que canta
> más de una escuela canta pensando en otras cosas . . .
>> (IV, xxxi, "El viento sobre Lincoln," The Wind
>>> over Lincoln)

At times the wind from the South rolls in / over the burial place of Lincoln carrying / voices and fragments of cities and trees / nothing happens at his tomb the letters do not move / the marble is softened with the slowness of centuries / the old gentleman no longer lives / the hole in his shirt no longer exists / the fibers of time and human dust have mixed / what a dedicated life murmurs a trembling / Virginia lady a school that sings / more than one school is singing while thinking about other things . . .

Neruda avails himself of these and many other diverse poetic procedures, some even pertaining to popular culture in his total effort to modulate every aspect of the poem, giving richness, variety, and a certain formal elegance to his general song of America. A section dealing with Zapata, peasant-hero of the Mexican Revolution, is organized around a popular tune, the well-known "Borrachita me voy":

Cuando arreciaron los dolores
en la tierra, y los espinares desolados
fueron la herencia de los campesinos,
y como antaño, las rapaces
barbas ceremoniales, y los látigos,
entonces, flor y fuego galopado . . .

> *Borrachita me voy*
> *hacia la capital*

se encabritó en el alba transitoria
la tierra sacudida de cuchillos,
el peón de sus amargas madrigueras
cayó como un elote desgranado
sobre la soledad vertiginosa.

> *a pedirle al patrón*
> *que me mandó llamar*

Zapata entonces fue tierra y aurora . . .
(IV, xxxiv, "A Emiliano Zapata con música de Tata Nacho,"
For Emiliano Zapata with music by Tata Nacho)

When the suffering grew in the land, and the barren brushlands, were the inheritance of the peasants, and as in yesteryear, the rapacious ceremonial beards, and the whips, then, flower and fire galloped . . .   *Tipsy I am going to the capital*   there rose up in the transitory dawn the land shaken by knives, the peasant from his bitter hovel fell like an ear of husked corn on the vertiginous solitude.   *to ask the master who ordered me to come*   Zapata then was the earth and the dawn . . .

The intercalated lyrics serve as a background for the principal narration, thus creating on the printed page a cinematic effect of simultaneity.

In yet another section, a popular musical form is used as the rhythmic base for the narrative itself. In a poem whose subject is Manuel Rodríguez, a Chilean guerrilla, the staccato measure of the *cueca,* a popular South American dance step, is pressed into service so as to mythify the figure's exploits:

Señora, dicen que donde,
mi madre dicen, dijeron
el agua y el viento dicen
que vieron al guerrillero.

Puede ser un obispo,
puede y no puede,
puede ser sólo el viento
sobre la nieve:
sobre la nieve, sí,
madre, no mires,
que viene galopando
Manuel Rodríguez.

Ya viene el guerrillero
por el estero ...

(IV, xxv, "Manuel Rodríguez")

Señora, they say where, my mother they say, they said, the water and the wind say that they saw the guerrilla.   It could be a bishop, it could and it could not, it could be only the wind on the snow: on the snow, yes, mother, don't look, for galloping this way is Manuel Rodriguez.   Now the guerrilla is coming through the pass ...

Not surprisingly, in Neruda's repertoire of poetizing procedures, familiar devices are preferred for they tend to naturalize the content of the text by inserting it in a known tradition. Thus, the stylized repetitions so characteristic of the Spanish "romance" are brought into play in a section dealing, appropriately, with Spain's prolonged war against the Araucanian Indians. The war against the Moors is thus transplanted to America:

Tres siglos estuvo luchando
la raza guerrera del roble,
trescientos años la centella

de Arauco pobló de cenizas
las cavidades imperiales.
Tres siglos cayeron heridas
las camisas del capitán,
trescientos años despoblaron
los arados y las colmenas,
trescientos años azotaron
cada nombre del invasor,
tres siglos rompieron la piel
de las águilas agresoras,
trescientos años enterraron
como la boca del océano
techos y huesos, armaduras,
torres y títulos dorados . . .

        (IV, xiii, "La dilatada guerra," The Drawn-Out War)

Three centuries did it battle the warrior race of oak, three hundred years the lightning of Arauco peopled with ashes the imperial cavities. Three centuries they fell down wounded the shirts of the captain, three hundred years they abandoned the plows and the beehives, three hundred years they lashed out at each name of the invader, three centuries they broke the skin of the aggressive eagles, three hundred years they buried like the mouth of an ocean roofs and bones, armaments, towers and gilded titles . . .

Humor too is used to capture and retain the interest of the reader, especially in portions of the poem dealing with the contemporary period. A decidedly revolutionary third-world sensibility is thus made engagingly acceptable to the relatively unpoliticized reader of 1950. Granted for a moment the effectiveness, or rather the persuasiveness, of Neruda's revision of the continent's past history, the primary purpose of *Canto general* was not to educate the public concerning the evils of the past but to create a political consciousness in order to assess the present situation. The poem's underlying theme is that tyranny is a corollary of the capitalist system and that, as the political and religious imperialism of Spain waned, it was replaced by the economic imperialism of England and then the United States, waging a modern-day crusade under the twin banners of progress and development. The problem is one of convincing the uncommitted reader of the day that he too is a part of the present system—a victim in fact—without unduly ridiculing him. Neruda's solution was eminently simple: engage the reader emotionally by ridiculing not him but the villain, foreign enterprise. The story of economic expansion in our time is therefore presented in a largely comic manner. A parody of the Second Coming heralds the multinationals' arrival on the scene as twentieth-century Savior:

> Cuando sonó la trompeta, estuvo
> todo preparado en la tierra,
> y Jehová repartió el mundo
> a Coca Cola Inc., Anaconda,
> Ford Motors, y otras entidades:
> la Compañía Frutera Inc.
> se reservó lo más jugoso . . .
> (V, ii, "La United Fruit Co," The United Fruit Company)

When the trumpet sounded, it was all prepared on the earth, and Jehovah distributed the world to Coca Cola Inc., Anaconda, Ford Motors, and other entities: the Fruit Company reserved for itself the juiciest part . . .

A new social order results, based on complicity between the national bourgeoisie and foreign enterprise. Low comedy is used to ridicule this society's most illustrious members, its politicians and diplomats. There is a burlesque sequence on how to be a puppet ambassador, a collage of clichés, which reads in part:

> Llámase Ud. Tonto Mengano,
> Tonto Joaquín Fernández, tonto
> Fulano de Tal, si es posible
> tenga una barba acrisolada.

Es todo cuanto se le exige
para "entablar negociaciones."
Informará después, sabihondo,
sobre su espectacular
presentación de credenciales,
diciendo: *Etc., la carroza,*
etc., Su Excelencia, etc.,
frases, etc., benévolas.

Tome una voz ahuecada y un
tono de vaca protectiva,
condecórese mutuamente
con el enviado de Trujillo . . .
(V, ii, "Diplomáticos, 1948," "Diplomats, 1948")

Call yourself Foolish Mengano, Foolish Joaquín Fernández, fool-
ish John Doe, if possible have a refined beard. That is all that
is required to "begin negotiating." You will report later,
deeply profound, about your spectacular presentation of cre-
dentials, saying: Etc., the carriage, etc. Your Excellency, etc.,
phrases, etc., benevolent.   Assume a solemn voice and a tone
of a protective cow, exchange decorations with the envoy of
Trujillo . . .

Even sections which read like white papers chronicling the
foreign companies' arrogant meddling in national affairs are
not exempt from an occasional note of humor. Laughter is a
useful alienating device, for it is always thought-provoking,
and once the reader recovers he must necessarily acknowledge
the underlying truth from which his amusement derives. An
opportunity for a sober reflective judgment soon follows in
Neruda's scheme of things. The ambassador is a fool, as is the
company representative; even more foolish though are the hol-
low entities they represent.

The Standard Oil chronicle begins with an account of pe-
troleum exploration, narrated in an elevated tone not unlike
that of a documentary (another form of propaganda). The
comic element is introduced midway through the narrative

sequence when the crude oil, discovered, becomes the personified subject of the poem; then, when the first drop of this animated substance peeps through the surface of the earth, it is greeted by a pallid representative of Standard Oil who of course ceremoniously claims it for the company:

> Cuando el barreno se abrió paso
> hacia las simas pedregales
> y hundió su intestino implacable
> en las haciendas subterráneas,
> y los años muertos, los ojos
> de las edades, las raíces
> de las plantas encarceladas
> y los sistemas escamosos
> se hicieron estratas del agua,
> subió por los tubos el fuego
> convertido en líquido frío,
> en la aduana de las alturas
> a la salida de su mundo
> de profundidad tenebrosa,
> encontró un pálido ingeniero
> y un título de propietario . . .
> (V, ii, "La Standard Oil Co.," The Standard Oil Company)

When the large borer opened a passage toward the rocky chasm and sunk its implacable intestine in the subterranean estates, and the dead years, the eyes of the ages, the roots of the imprisoned plants and scaly systems became strata of water, there ran up through the tubes fire converted into cold liquid, in the customs house of the heights at the exit from its world of dark profundity, it was met by a pallid engineer and a certificate of ownership . . .

The familiar logo of the company and its propietary omnipresence also makes for an ironic, if not entirely whimsical, ending to an otherwise sad tale of international interventionism. Bolivia and Paraguay, two of the continent's poorest countries, send their Indian foot-soldiers off to battle over which nation has the right to award oil contracts for the jungles of the Chaco, whose borders they share. Gulf and Standard Oil are the real belligerents in the Chaco War (1932–1935). Standard Oil wins:

> Un presidente asesinado
> por una gota de petróleo,
> una hipoteca de millones
> de hectáreas, un fusilamiento
> rápido en una mañana
> mortal de luz, petrificada,
> un nuevo campo de presos
> subversivos, en Patagonia,
> una traición, un tiroteo
> bajo la luna petrolada,
> un cambio sutil de ministros
> en la capital, un rumor
> como una marea de aceite,
> y luego el zarpazo, y verás
> cómo brillan, sobre las nubes,
> sobre los mares, en tu casa,
> las letras de la Standard Oil
> iluminando sus dominios.

A president assassinated for a drop of petroleum, a mortgage on millions of acres, a quick firing squad in a mortal morning of light, petrified, a new camp for subversive prisoners, in Patagonia, a treason, a shootout under the petroleated moon, a subtle change of ministers in the capital, a rumor rises like a high tide of oil, and then the master stroke, and you see how they glow, over the clouds, over the seas, in your house, the logo of Sandard Oil illuminating its domain.

In this way, through abundant humor and irony, multiple narrative points of view, and with a plethora of mystical, lyrical, and rhetorical devices, the reader of *Canto general* is manipulated aesthetically and plied ideologically in Neruda's five-hundred-page effort to win him over to the cause. No amount of textual explication can hope to do complete justice to the richness and diversity of this lengthy major work. Similarly, no amount of bibliographical data can ever determine exactly the effectiveness of this text as literary propaganda. We can only identify some of the artistic procedures and indicate how they function in relation to the book's content. In this context, it is only fair to add that Neruda's epic, partly because of its extraordinary length, but mostly because of its controversial content, was soon cannibalized by diverse literary establishments for no less diverse and conflicting purposes. And so it is that most nonspecialist readers of Neruda today know *Canto general* only partially, through "representative" selections.

It is ironic that the poet's first truly sustained effort to create a cyclical epic embracing the social history of the people of this continent, written expressly for them and narrated as though by them, is so imperfectly known by its intended public: the ordinary man. As Neruda told the editor of *Books Abroad* at the outset of the project, in 1940, "to write for the people is too great an ambition." Perhaps it is in recognition of this fact that Neruda's next poetic venture turned out to be so different, less ambitious, more ordinary, simple, and elegiac: a series of "elementary odes" written for a daily newspaper, later to become the volume of *Odas elementales* (1954).

6. Plain Lyricism
Odas elementales

> Poetry is like bread, and it must be shared by every-
> one, the men of letters and the peasants, by everyone
> in our vast, incredible, extraordinary family of man.
> I confess that to write simply has been my most diffi-
> cult task.
>
> *1953*

In 1954 Pablo Neruda published two quite different books of
poetry, *Odas elementales* (Elementary Odes) and *Las uvas y
el viento* (The Grapes and the Wind). Either one, if taken
separately, might well seem to be an illustration of the ideal-
istic premise contained in the epigraph above: that poetry,
like bread, is a product for all the people, the cosmopolitan
as well as the provincial. Yet only one of the two books proved
to be successful on a large scale before such a heterogeneous
public.

   Las uvas y el viento (Santiago, Nascimento), all but forgot-
ten today, was a kind of sequel to *Canto general*. It presented
an updated poematic narrative of the author's bedazzled per-
egrination through Eastern Europe, behind what was then
called the "Iron Curtain." The effort was totally unconvincing
(except in the Soviet Union which, in 1953, had awarded him
the Stalin Peace Prize). Neruda, later acknowledging his fail-
ure to reach a wider audience with this book, offered the opin-
ion that it was perhaps too bluntly political: *"Las uvas y el
viento,* a poem of geographical and political content, was in
some ways a frustrated effort . . . Its geographical range and its

inevitable political passion made it difficult for many of my readers to accept."*

Odas elementales (Buenos Aires, Losada), on the other hand, was quite different. Political without appearing to be politicized, simple without being simplistic, it appealed to an extraordinarily wide range of readers through a seemingly artless, almost breezy series of compositions exalting the most basic things of our daily existence, the plain and the ordinary, fruits and flowers, thread and bread. Neruda's poetic posture in the odes, while deliberately naive, was not without a certain sophistication. To reach a new audience, supposedly unfamiliar with the conventions of poetry, without alienating the old was envisaged as a delicate affair. Accordingly, the reader finds sprinkled throughout *Odas elementales* poems directed toward the critics, the supposedly effete arbiters of literary taste whose reaction to simple poetry was anticipated to be both negative and hostile. Whether these poems were originally conceived as preventive measures designed to neutralize one kind of reader or as seductive placebos for a mass readership is impossible to ascertain at this point. The reaction of the present-day reader to poems like "Oda a la crítica" (Ode to the Critics) or "Oda a la sencillez" (Ode to Simplicity) is one of pleasant amusement. In the pointedly titled ode to simplicity, for example, Neruda uses the broad stroke of the caricaturist to hold up to ridicule those who would criticize the plainness of his new poetry:

> Sencillez, te pregunto:
> me acompañaste siempre?
> O te vuelvo a encontrar
> en mi silla, sentada?
> Ahora
> no quieren aceptarme
> contigo,
> me miran de reojo,

* "Algunas reflexiones," *Mapocho*, 2:182 (1964).

se preguntan quién es
la pelirroja.
El mundo,
mientras nos encontrábamos
y nos reconocíamos,
se llenaba de tontos
tenebrosos,
de hijos de fruta tan repletos
de palabras
como los diccionarios,
tan llenos de viento
como una tripa que nos quiere hacer
y ahora que llegamos
después de tantos viajes
desentonamos
en la poesía.
Sencillez, qué terrible lo que nos pasa:
no quieren recibirnos
en los salones,
los cafés están llenos
de los más exquisitos
pederastas,
y tú y yo nos miramos,
no nos quieren ...
una mala jugada

Simplicity, I ask you: were you with me always? Or do I again
find you in my chair, seated? Now they won't accept me with you,
they look at me askance, they ask themselves who is the redhead.
The world, while we were getting together and getting reac-
quainted, was filling up with gloomy fools, with sons of a fruit
as replete with words as the dictionaries, as full of wind as a
stomach that wants to play us a dirty trick and now that we are
arriving after so many trips we are in disharmony with poetry.
Simplicity, how terrible is what is happening to us: they don't
want to admit us in the salons, the cafes are filled with the most
exquisite pederasts, and you and I look at each other, they don't
want us...

The varied length of the lines, with some verses as short as
a single word, is disconcerting at first. The effect, though, is

ultimately compelling, for when the composition is read through, line by halting line, the rhythmic result tends to accentuate the prosaic quality of the discourse, making it seem more natural, almost plainspoken, hence less "poetic." At the same time, the reading process being what it is—an intrinsically reflective act of intellection—the text in its printed form is a constant visual signal that the poem is a literary creation; the uniform left-hand margin and the overall blankness of the page frame the words, setting them apart as having been especially chosen. The "Ode to Simplicity" is, in the final analysis, a verbal composition, a structured discourse—an artful defense of plainness.

Curiously enough, such a defense was really not necessary, for *Odas elementales* turned out to be an immediate and unqualified success with practically everyone, the ordinary reader as well as the literary establishment. Even potentially hostile critics who had once been put off by the politicized author of *Tercera residencia* and *Canto general,* not to mention *Las uvas y el viento,* marveled over the candor and clarity of these simple odes. The arch-conservative Alone (Hernán Díaz Arrieta), who had helped Neruda get started in the 1920s but later parted ways with him over politics, was not untypical in his warm and forgiving response:

> Some say this clarity of expression was imposed by the Soviets so that Neruda would be able to reach the masses. If that were true, we would have to forgive the Soviets for an awful lot . . . Bitterness gone, complex obscurity banished, it was to fear that poetry would reach excessively down to the lowest common denominator and fall into prose. Well, never has the poetry of Neruda seemed more authentic . . . We would like to place a limit on this praise. It is said that no judgment is good without its reservations. But we can find none. We even forgive the poet his Communism.*

* "Muerte y transfiguración de Pablo Neruda," *El Mercurio* (Santiago), January 30, 1955.

The academic critics were equally enthusiastic. Even those who were disturbed by the apparent formlessness of Neruda's flexible poetic line, by what appeared to be a river of print running down the center of the page, were nonetheless resourcefully encomiastic in their critiques. One scholar even went so far as to rearrange some lines in order to show that the odes were primarily classical in structure and not really free verse at all,* as though the ostensibly "real" form of the ode was somehow purposefully dispersed by Neruda in an effort not to seem too highbrow.

All in all, the poet could do no wrong with his *Odas elementales*. So he promptly set about to do more of the same, penning three more volumes for Losada: *Nuevas odas elementales* (New Elementary Odes) in 1956; *Tercer libro de las odas* (The Third Book of Odes) in 1957; and *Navegaciones y regresos* (Voyages and Homecomings), subtitled "el cuarto volumen de las *Odas elementales*" (the fourth volume of the Elementary Odes), in 1959. For many readers of the time, this literary phenomenon seemed to be repeating, in a somewhat more compressed time period, that of *Residencia en la tierra,* a multivolume series of poems which, taken together, constitute a cycle. In retrospect, however, the odes, unlike the poetry of the *Residencia* cycle, reveal no significant pattern of change. The literary form and the thematic focus, once fixed in the first volume, varied little throughout the rest of the series. Even for Neruda, normally eager to point out every nuance of change in his work, all four books are considered as one:

> These odes, because of an outside stimulus, were transformed into something that I was always after: an extended and total poem. The initial stimulus came from a newspaper in Caracas, *El Nacional,* whose director, my dear friend Miguel Otero Silva, asked me to contribute a weekly column of poetry. I ac-

* "Well, if Neruda titles his compositions *odas,* it is because they are really written in verses of seven and eleven syllables." Luis García-Abrines, "La forma en la última poesía de Neruda," *Revista Hispánica Moderna,* 25:304 (October 1959).

cepted, asking only that this collaboration of mine not be published in the Arts page of the literary supplement . . . but in the news section. In this way, I managed to publish a history of the time, of diverse things, trades, people, fruits, and flowers, of life and my vision, of the struggle, in fact of all that I could take in through this vast cyclic urge of my creation. I think therefore of all the *Odas elementales* as a single book.*

In this retrospective view, everything is compressed—perhaps too much. The fact of the matter is that of the almost two hundred and fifty poems contained in the four books of odes only a handful were ever published in *El Nacional.* So it was not the pressure of a weekly deadline that kept him going, but rather the idea of a newspaper column and its vast circulation with a predictable readership that prompted him to work out a plainer, more public literary style. Whatever the motivation, the result was the same: the universally successful elementary, or elemental, ode.

The first such poem was published in *El Nacional* on October 16, 1952. An anticipation of "Oda al hombre sencillo" (Ode to the Simple Man), its genre then was not specified in the title. More important at the time was its linguistic level, its use of everyday language, the spoken language of the people. Thus, the poem's original title, "Hablando en la calle" (Talking in the Street), was in itself a programmatic announcement. Appropriately enough, its tone was intimately conversational, even conspiratorial:

> Voy a contarte en secreto
> quién soy yo,
> así, en voz alta,
> me dirás quién eres,
> quiero saber quién eres,
> cuánto ganas,
> en qué taller trabajas,
> en qué mina,

* "Algunas reflexiones," p. 182.

en qué farmacia,
tengo una obligación terrible
y es saberlo,
saberlo todo,
día y noche saber
cómo te llamas,
ése es mi oficio,
conocer una vida
no es bastante
ni conocer todas las vidas
es necesario,
verás,
hay que desentrañar,
rascar a fondo
y como en una tela
las líneas ocultaron,
con el color, la trama
del tejido,
yo borro los colores
y busco hasta encontrar
el tejido profundo,
así también encuentro
la unidad de los hombres,
y en el pan
busco
más allá de la forma:
me gusta el pan, lo muerdo,
y entonces
veo el trigo,
los trigales tempranos,
la verde forma de la primavera,
las raíces, el agua,
por eso
más allá del pan,
veo la tierra,
la unidad de la tierra,
el agua,
el hombre,
y así todo lo pruebo

buscándote
en todo.
Ando, nado, navego
hasta encontrarte,
y entonces te pregunto
cómo te llamas,
calle y número,
para que tú recibas
mis cartas,
para que yo te diga
quién soy y cuánto gano,
dónde vivo,
y cómo era mi padre.
Ves tú qué simple soy,
qué simple eres,
no se trata
de nada complicado,
yo trabajo contigo,
tú vives, vas y vienes
de un lado a otro,
es muy sencillo:
eres la vida,
eres tan transparente
como el agua,
y así soy yo,
mi obligación es ésa:
ser transparente,
cada día
me educo,
cada día me peino
pensando como piensas,
y ando
como tú andas,
como, como tú comes
tengo en mis brazos a mi amor
como a tu novia tú,
y entonces
cuando esto está probado,
cuando somos iguales

escribo,
escribo con tu vida y con la mía,
con tu amor y los míos,
con todos tus dolores
y entonces
ya somos diferentes
porque, mi mano en tu hombro,
como viejos amigos
te digo en las orejas:
no sufras,
ya llega el día,
ven,
ven conmigo,
ven
con todos
los que a ti se parecen,
los más sencillos,
ven,
no sufras,
ven conmigo,
porque aunque no lo sepas,
eso yo sí lo sé:
y sé hacia dónde vamos,
y es ésta la palabra:
no sufras
porque ganaremos,
ganaremos nosotros,
los más sencillos,
ganaremos,
aunque tú no lo creas,
ganaremos.

I am going to tell you in secret who I am, thus, out loud, you will tell me who you are, how much you make, in which shop you work, in which mine, in which pharmacy, I have a terrible obligation and it is to know, to know everything, day and night to know what you call yourself, that is my job, to know a life is not enough nor is it necessary to know all lives, you will see, it is necessary to dig out, to scratch below and as in a canvas the lines hidden by color, the pattern of the weave, I erase the colors and I search until finding the deep weave, thus I also find the unity of men, and in bread I search beyond form: I like bread, I bite into it, and then I see wheat, the early wheat fields, the green form of Spring, roots, water, for this reason beyond bread, I see the earth, the unity of the earth, water, man, and in this way I try everything looking for you in everything. I walk, I swim, I sail until I find you, and then I ask your name, street and number, so that you can receive my letters, so that I can tell you who I am and how much I make, where I live, and what my father was like. See how simple I am, how simple you are, it is not a question of anything complicated, I work with you, you live, you come and go, from one place to another, it is very simple: you are life, you are as transparent as water, and so am I, my obligation is this: to be transparent, each day I educate myself, each day I comb my hair thinking as you think, and I walk as you walk, I eat, as you eat, I have my love in my arms as you your girlfriend, and then when this is proven, when we are equals I write, I write with your life and mine, with your love and mine, with all your pains and then we are already different because, my hand on your shoulder, like old friends I will say to your ears: don't suffer, the day is already coming, come come with me, come with all those that are like you, the simplest, come, don't suffer, come with me, because even though you don't know it, I certainly do: and I know just where we are heading, and this is the word: don't suffer because we're going to win, we shall win, the simplest, we're going to win, even though you don't believe it, we're going to win.

The poem begins well enough, but as it goes on, the discursive situation—talking in the street—seems forced. The speaker's self-consciousness ("ves tú qué simple soy," see how simple I am) and political optimism ("aunque tú no lo creas, ganaremos," even though you don't believe it, we're going to win), carryovers from *Canto general*, weigh the text down. In subsequent compositions of this type Neruda would jettison what here seems like mere rhetorical ballast and utilize the ode more successfully as a plain eulogistic form. In doing so he would retain the most arresting qualities of "Hablando en la calle": its everyday language and the stretched-out columnar form of its presentation.

The disjointed and distended phrase, so visually impressive to readers of *Odas elementales* in 1954, may well have had its origin in the newspaper format, in the necessity to compress each line into a limited space. Be that as it may, this was the form Neruda was to employ in all four books of odes, the form which ultimately proved to be so appropriate to his new role of citizen-poet, purportedly speaking to no one in particular but in fact philosophizing to the world about practically everything. In this manner, somewhat like an artistic utility, Neruda managed to go completely public, to make his poetry perform a useful service. That the literary vehicle for carrying out this public service turned out to be the ode is not surprising, since this form has by tradition been reserved for civic poetry. Neruda had experimented with it before (the 1938 "Oda de invierno al río Mapocho" comes immediately to mind), but it was only with the loose versification and the conversational diction of his seemingly revolutionary *Odas elementales* that he was finally able to reach that vast public he had so long been striving to communicate with. In the process he thoroughly transformed his poetic expression, once again renewing both its style and its content.

Originally the ode was a special sort of poem, a vehicle of praise and exultation, destined to be sung in public. The Pindaric ode was civic in nature, the Horation ode was lyrical. And poets since the Renaissance have imitated now Pindar, now Horace. In Spanish this was almost always done in *silvas* or *liras,* a variable combination of verses of seven and eleven syllables, first used by Garcilaso and generally thought to capture best the metrical irregularity of the classical ode. Neruda's *Odas elementales* depart from this established modality with a highly flexible free verse form and a unique thematic focus that strives to be both public and lyrical— and elemental.

In point of fact, what drew the most critical fire was not the form of the odes but their subject matter. For the unsophisticated reader they were too unorthodox in content. Odes to the ordinary seemed "unpoetic." Yet, even the prim Ronsard composed an ode to his bed, Keats to an urn, Shelley to the wind, and Andrés Bello to tropical farming. So it is not unusual as such that a poet should write on his surroundings, banal though they may be. What is unusual is that he should deal almost exclusively with the elemental and the ordinary, even perhaps the trivial; all together, subjects like fish-soup, onions, and socks seem rather too slight for the solemn tradition of the ode. But these subjects are slight in name only, and that is their charm, for Neruda treats them with the same reverence that Saint Francis of Assisi had for all of God's creation in his *Cantico delle creature,* and with the same sense of marvel that the Spanish Fray Luis de Granada had for even the most insignificant of these creatures—fish, houseflies, and ants were fit subjects for his literature in the service of Christianity. So they would be for Neruda's modern-day cause. After *Canto general* the poet, without abandoning his social commitment, began to take on in earnest the very philosophic pose he had so roundly rejected in his more youthful poetry; now, at fifty, we find him benignly celebrating practically everything that comes his way, even, for example, something as obviously fortuitous as a chestnut fallen to the ground:

> Del follaje erizado
> caíste
> completa,
> de madera pulida,
> de lúcida caoba,
> lista
> como un violín que acaba
> de nacer en la altura,
> y cae
> ofreciendo sus dones encerrados,
> su escondida dulzura,

terminado en secreto
entre pájaros y hojas,
escuela de la forma,
linaje de la leña y de la harina,
instrumento ovalado
que guarda en su estructura
delicia intacta y rosa comestible.
En lo alto abandonaste
el erizado erizo
que entreabrió sus espinas
en la luz del castaño,
por esa partidura
viste el mundo,
pájaros
llenos de sílabas,
rocío
con estrellas,
y abajo
cabezas de muchachos
y muchachas,
hierbas que tiemblan sin reposo,
humo que sube y sube.
Te decidiste,
castaña,
y saltaste a la tierra,
bruñida y preparada,
endurecida y suave
como un pequeño seno
de las islas de América.
Caíste
golpeando
el suelo
pero
nada pasó,
la hierba
siguió temblando, el viejo
castaño susurró como las bocas
de toda una arboleda,
cayó una hoja del otoño rojo,

firme siguieron trabajando
las horas en la tierra.
Porque eres
sólo
una semilla,
castaño, otoño, tierra,
agua, altura, silencio
prepararon el germen,
la harinosa espesura,
los párpados maternos
que abrirán, enterrados,
de nuevo hacia la altura
la magnitud sencilla
de un follaje,
la oscura trama húmeda
de unas nuevas raíces,
las antiguas y nuevas dimensiones
de otro castaño en la tierra.

("Oda a una castaña en el suelo," Ode to a
Chestnut on the Ground)

From the bristled foliage you fell complete, of polished wood, shiny mahogany, ready like a violin which has just been born in the heights, and falls offering its covered gifts, its hidden sweetness, perfected in secret among birds and leaves, school of form, lineage of firewood and flour, oval instrument that keeps in its structure virgin delight, and edible rose. Up there you abandoned the bristly husk that half-opened its spines in the light of the chestnut tree, through that opening you saw the world, birds brimming with syllables, dew with stars, and below heads of boys and girls, grass that trembles without rest, fumes that rise and rise. You decided, chestnut, and you leaped to earth, burnished and ready, firm and soft like a tiny nipple of the islands of America. You fell hitting the ground but nothing happened, the grass kept on trembling, the old chestnut tree whispered along with the mouths of the whole grove, a leaf from red autumn fell, impassive the earth's hours went on working. Because you are only a seed, chestnut tree, autumn, earth, water, height, silence prepared the germ, the floury thickness, the ma-

ternal eyelids that will open, buried, again towards the height
the simple majesty of foliage, the damp dark plot of new roots,
the old and new dimensions of another chestnut tree on the
earth.

This is one of the book's briefer compositions, made up of
just five declarative sentences. Thus, in a few straightforward
phrases, Neruda manages to transform a subject which on the
surface seems frivolous into something sublime. Fundamental
to this accomplishment is a basic procedural pattern found in
most of the *Odas elementales,* a pattern of enunciation, trans-
formation, and ratiocination. At the outset of each poem the
elemental subject so extravagantly announced by the title is
promptly metaphorized so as to accord it a certain level of
poetic dignity; the oval shape and the brown color of the
chestnut are associated with polished mahogany and a violin,
elegant and noble points of comparison for a simple *castaña.*
Further into the poem, the subject is more completely trans-
formed; the chestnut is personified, and instead of simply fall-
ing to the ground as in the first telling, it is seen to leap down
voluntarily so as to partake of life's activities. Finally, in the
conclusion, the poem takes on a philosophic dimension as the
speaker reasons on the significance of the elemental; the ig-
nored chestnut has a grand destiny: it is a seed and is to be-
come a tree.

Such poematic philosophizing would seem a bit simplistic
in an age such as ours were it not for the fact that the poet-
philosopher in this case is not just any writer, but Pablo
Neruda. The accomplished author in his mature years has
earned the privilege of writing simply and being taken seri-
ously. This was not always so. It was once the other way around.
The thirty-year-old author of *Residencia en la tierra* had reso-
lutely foresworn the role of interpreter of life's mysteries in
order to achieve a greater poetic realism; now, at fifty, and
serenely confident of his articulatory powers, he seems com-
fortable in the adopted role of philosopher. Accordingly, his

elementary odes are more explicitly interpretative than any of his previous poetry.

There is a fundamental difference between the treatment of patently similar themes in, say, the "Cantos materiales" of 1935 and the *Odas elementales* of 1954. Both poetize the ordinary, but the *Residencia* poems were self-centered, exclusively concerned with the personal significance of wood, wine, and celery for the anguished existential author: it was the speaker of "Entrada a la madera" who had a mystic experience with wood; in "Estatuto del vino" it was the poet's life that would somehow be richer because he could appreciate the pleasure of drunkenness; and in "Apogeo del apio," even the life-giving celery came to him in a dream. We readers were always somewhat outside the system, mere spectators whose function was to be awed as we reverentially admired the poet and his extraordinary experiences with the ordinary. In *Odas elementales* the situation is reversed; the poem is designed to involve us in the process of intellection, hence the importance of the pattern of enunciation, transformation, and ratiocination. The poem is designed as a didactic artifice, helping us to see, to witness, and to speculate on the marvelous significance of the world in which we live, all of us. For this reason, the elementary ode almost always ends sententiously, with a kind of philosophic maxim summarizing the lesson, an epiphonema to help the reader grasp the poem's practical import. Neruda wanted each composition to have a conceptual handle, and in the preface to the second book of odes, *Nuevas odas elementales,* he even spelled it out as such:

> Quiero que todo
> tenga
> empuñadura,
> que todo sea
> taza o herramienta.
> ("La casa de las odas," The House of Odes)

I want everything to have a handle, everything to be a cup or a tool.

The image is at once strange and familiar. This is because, some twenty years before, in another declaration of principles, "Sobre una poesía sin pureza," Neruda had also spoken of tools. At that time his concern with realism in poetry had led him to ponder the aesthetic value of ordinary objects, most especially the utilitarian: "It is very convenient, at certain times of the day or night, to observe deeply objects at rest: the wheels that have covered long, dusty distances . . . the handles and grips of the tools of a carpenter. The contact of man with the universe issues from these things like a lesson for the tortured lyric poet."*

Twenty years later, poetry itself is to be the tool with a handle, and the lesson it issues is not just for the poet but for everyone. "Tortured" lyricism is a relic of the past. The change in attitude is important, for it permits us to appreciate the strikingly differing treatments of the ordinary object in "Cantos materiales" and *Odas elementales*. Essentially, the difference is functional: the difference between poetry as a vehicle for communicable discourse and poetry as a device for hermetic self-expression; the difference between what the object means to the poet as a unique individual and what it ultimately means to us, the readers; the difference, in short, between personal and public lyricism.

Although the turnabout was complete, it was neither sudden nor capricious. *Odas elementales* is, in a very real sense, a logical corollary of *Canto general,* the lyric counterpart of the public voice Neruda had earlier assumed for the narrative purpose of the epic. Only the tone is somewhat more subdued, for the philosophic speaker of the odes is necessarily less spectacular than was the many-voiced narrator of the general song of America. Appropriately enough, the volume's introductory poem, a kind of *ars poetica* for Neruda's odic style, is entitled "El hombre invisible" (Invisible Man). From a generative point of view the poem is doubly important for it was

* *Caballo Verde para la Poesía,* I, 1 (October 1935).

first made public in November 1952, scarcely a month after "Hablando en la calle" had been wedged into the columns of *El Nacional.* Furthermore, it was originally published not in the Caracas newspaper, but in *Pro-Arte,* a sophisticated Chilean literary review of rather predictable circulation. Neruda was evidently broaching with some care and not a little trepidation the recurrent subject of change in his poetry. Hence we find the studied whimsicality of the contrast made between the new order and the old, between the personal and the public functions of the lyric poet:

> Yo me río,
> me sonrío
> de los viejos poetas,
> yo adoro toda
> la poesía escrita,
> todo el rocío,
> luna, diamante, gota
> de plata sumergida,
> que fue mi antiguo hermano,
> agregando a la rosa,
> pero
> me sonrío,
> siempre dicen "yo,"
> a cada paso
> les sucede algo,
> es siempre "yo,"
> por las calles
> sólo ellos andan
> o la dulce que aman,
> nadie más,
> no pasan pescadores,
> ni libreros,
> no pasan albañiles,
> nadie se cae
> de un andamio,
> nadie sufre,
> nadie ama,

sólo mi pobre hermano,
el poeta,
a él le pasan
todas las cosas
y a su dulce querida,
nadie vive
sino él solo . . .

I laugh, I smile at the old poets, I adore all written poetry, all the dew, moon, diamond, drop of submerged silver, that my old brother was adding on to the rose, but I smile, they always say "I," with each step something happens to them, it is always "I," through the streets only they walk or the sweet thing they love, no one else, fishermen don't pass by, nor book-vendors, brick-layers don't pass by, no one falls from the scaffold, no one suffers, no one loves, only my poor brother, the poet, to him happens everything and to his sweet lover, no one lives except him alone . . .

For the lettered reader of *Pro-Arte* in 1952, familiar only with Neruda's past work and the many permutations effected in his aesthetic system over the years, this poem was an almost too-familiar harbinger of change. Neruda's tendency to shed his past poetics like a snake its skin, and to emerge each time seemingly renewed yet fundamentally the same was becoming something of a topos. So it was not until 1954 that the poem was finally accorded its proper importance; it appeared then as the introductory text to *Odas elementales,* setting forth the aesthetic precepts of Neruda's extraordinary new book. In this integral context what is actually new in the poet's attitude can be seen to be much more important than the whimsical critique of his past "errors." Midway through the poem Neruda tempers the derision of his former literary self and, alluding to the title ("El hombre invisible"), brings the lyric poet down from the heights of Parnassus to street level, to what turns out to be the public plane of the elementary ode:

Yo no soy superior
a mi hermano

pero sonrío,
porque voy por las calles
y sólo yo no existo,
la vida corre
como todos los ríos,
yo soy el único
invisible . . .

I am not superior to my brother but I smile, because I go
through the streets and only I do not exist, life runs on like all
the rivers, I am the only one invisible . . .

For its obliqueness, this is a far more persuasive statement of
the author's newfound sensibility than that contained earlier
in "Hablando en la calle" ("ves tú qué simple soy"). Both texts,
however, composed at approximately the same point in time
(October–November 1952), announce without equivocation an
unusually public role for the normally introspective voice of
the lyric poet. Like the many-voiced narrator of *Canto general,*
the odic poet is also a performer; his audience is to be the com-
mon man and so he must speak in the everyday language of
the people. For this the poet as plain-speaker must abandon
his claim to uniqueness as an artist and recognize his genuine
ordinariness as one man among many; as a modern-day poet
of the people he is now to be, in a word, *invisible.*

The obvious danger with such a role is that the poetry it
produces might seem not merely simple but simplistic and
therefore not to be taken seriously. But this did not happen
with Neruda's *Odas elementales* when the book first appeared
in 1954, and it is interesting to ponder why. For one thing, the
book form itself may have obviated such an attitude, although
only minimally it would seem. More importantly, Hispanic
poetry had begun to change, reflecting in part the innovative
sway of other literatures, specifically that of the United States
whose plainspoken writers of the "beat" generation had more
than a local impact. In Chile by 1954 Nicanor Parra had al-
ready brought out a significant part of the anti-poetry he was

to collect later that same year in *Poemas y antipoemas*. Parra and the beat writers had removed poetry from its genteel tradition. Neruda made it humble and people-oriented. Paradoxically, Neruda's success with humility also derives from the fact that, as was said before, he was Neruda, mid-century giant of Hispanic literature. His latest "conversion," therefore, seemed epochal. Like Picasso, he had the uncanny ability to perceive change and to place himself in the vanguard. There was of course some harping of Neruda at the time but it had no effect. Pablo de Rokha, an erstwhile rival, even brought out an entire book in 1955, denying Neruda's originality. The book, pompously and belligerently titled *Neruda y Yo* was generally ignored, not because the thesis was totally untenable, but simply unwanted. Time had given Neruda a stature that could not be diminished, neither by the flailing denigrations of a Pablo de Rokha, nor even by the poet's own repeated declarations of his ordinariness. Simplicity gave him a new grandeur.

Whereas the younger Parra was aggressively sardonic in his antipoetry, the mature Neruda could afford to be benign; and while the indefatigable Pablo de Rokha frantically fussed about what was wrong with his rival and the world, Pablo Neruda went on serenely celebrating what was right. It seemed for a time as though Neruda was heralding a new Age of Reason. In fact, if there is a single characteristic which overrides all others in *Odas elementales,* it is the speaker's serendipity, his tendency to make everything ultimately seem agreeable. Neruda had promised as much in the declaration of principles contained in "El hombre invisible." For that poem's conclusion he had even updated a Romantic formula for poetry so as to highlight his intention to use literature not as an aesthetic end in itself, but as a means to achieve a greater end. Suffering was to be transformed not into poesy, but hope:

> Dadme todo el dolor
> de todo el mundo,

yo voy a transformarlo
en esperanza.

Give me all the pain of everyone, I am going to transform it into
hope.

Accordingly, there are odes to sadness, intranquillity, and soli-
tude in which these topics—standbys of the lyric repertory
since time immemorial—are flamboyantly laid to rest:

Enterraré, tristeza, tus huesos roedores
bajo la primavera de un manzano.
("Oda a la tristeza," Ode to Sadness)

I shall bury, sadness, your gnawing bones under the Spring of an
apple tree.

Conversely, there are odes to happiness, tranquillity, and
togetherness in which these themes are treated as though they
were somehow unique—and so appear to have been unearthed
by the modern lyricist with a public conscience:

Te desdeñé, alegría.
Fui mal aconsejado.
La luna
me llevó por sus caminos.
Los antiguos poetas
me prestaron anteojos
y junto a cada cosa
un nimbo oscuro
puse,
sobre la flor una corona negra,
sobre la boca amada
un triste beso.
Aún es temprano.
Déjame arrepentirme.
("Oda a la alegría," Ode to Happiness)

I disdained you, happiness. I was poorly counseled. The moon carried me along its path. The ancient poets lent me spectacles and next to each thing I placed a dark halo, on the flower a black crown, on the mouth of the loved one a sad kiss. It is still early. Let me repent.

Much of this is pure bluff, but it works. And in art that is what counts. Neruda situates himself so as to look at the same old world from a new perspective, a perspective that permits him to be boldly irreverent with his own work and the tradition from which it derives. In the process he reworks some of the oldest clichés of literature. Autumn, for example, perennial symbol of waning and decay, is given a new life:

> Modesto es el otoño
> como los leñadores.
> Cuesta mucho
> sacar todas las hojas
> de todos los árboles
> de todos los países.
> La primavera
> las cosió volando
> y ahora
> hay que dejarlas
> caer como si fueran
> pájaros amarillos.
> No es fácil.
> Hace falta tiempo.
> Hay que correr por todos
> los caminos,
> hablar idiomas,
> sueco,
> portugués,
> hablar en lengua roja,
> en lengua verde.
> Hay que saber
> callar en todos
> los idiomas

y en todas partes,
siempre,
dejar caer,
caer,
dejar caer,
caer
las hojas.

("Oda al otoño," Ode to Autumn)

Autumn is modest like the woodcutters. It is difficult to take down all the leaves from all the trees of all the countries. Spring stitched them together on the wing and now they must be allowed to fall as though they were yellow birds. It is not easy. Time is needed. It is necessary to run through all the roads of the world, to speak many languages, Swedish, Portuguese, to speak with a red tongue a green tongue. It is necessary to know how to shut up in every language and everywhere, always, allow to fall, to fall, to allow to fall, to fall the leaves.

Here, simple repetition and the abbreviated line are used to advantage, giving a visual stress to the falling leaves. Autumn is not to be sadly dreaded, but anxiously awaited.

The poet's attitude is so consistently serendipitous throughout the volume's sixty-seven odes, that the book, taken as a whole, is much less convincing than its individual compositions. The overall effect is like that of a fairy tale: we are charmed by each fantastic occurrence but unwilling to accept the overall design as a meaningful facsimile of reality. The poems were really meant to be experienced individually, sampled in a random fashion, not read through from cover to cover as with *Canto general*—and, most especially not grouped together and schematized as I am doing here for the purpose of a more succinct and orderly exposition. In fact, the odes are not at all meaningfully arranged in the book; they follow one another alphabetically according to title. The result is one of ordered *dis*-order.

Written independently, and published separately in diverse

167

reviews over a two-year period, each ode is meant to stand alone. Its true literary context is not the other odes but all of Neruda's previous poetry. The "Oda al día feliz" (Ode to a Happy Day), for example, alludes to the somber side of Neruda's earlier poetry and even makes pointed use of a formulaic expression from one of the *Residencia* poems. Whereas in 1935 the world-weary speaker of "Walking around"could only bring himself to say "sucede que me canso de ser hombre," now the benign philosopher uses the same conversational gambit to announce his happiness:

> Esta vez dejadme
> ser feliz,
> nada ha pasado a nadie,
> no estoy en parte alguna,
> sucede solamente
> que soy feliz . . .

> This time let me be happy, nothing has happened to anyone, I am not anywhere, it just happens that I am happy . . .

This insistence on happiness and the poet's thematic preference for the little things of daily life had a double-acting effect on the reader: immediate enthrallment followed by gradual disenchantment, even disbelief.

Neruda's program in the odes was ingenuously simple: to speak to the people in the language of the people about people-oriented things. This is the counterpart and corollary of *Canto general*. The macrocosmic view of the principal speaker in the epic poem is exchanged for a minute attention to detail, for a microcosmic view in the elementary odes. Nothing is gratuitous. Everything is examined not for its hidden beauty but for its everyday function, the real use to which it is put. This is totally different from the Horation concept of mixing the useful and the beautiful (*utile dulci*), and in a poem like the exotic "Oda a la cebolla" (Ode to the Onion), the ordinary onion is transformed into something extraordinary, not by the poet's fantasy alone, but by the use man customarily makes of it. A comparison may be helpful. Neoclassic poets made frequent use of the odic form to elevate the humble, to attribute a certain dignity to the ordinary. In Latin America, for example, there are many eighteenth-century odes to the fruits and vegetables of the New World. One of these, Manuel de Zequeira's well-known ode to pineapple ("A la piña"), exalts the exotic fruit by placing it in a classical setting: Jupiter comes to the New World to fetch some pineapple juice for the gods back on Mt. Olympus. The humble pineapple is made worthy by association. Its cultivation is imaginatively described by the Cuban colonial poet in this highly conjectural way:

Del seno fértil de la madre tierra,
en actitud erguida se levanta
la airosa piña de esplandor vestida,
llena de ricas galas.

Desde que nace, liberal Pomona
con la muy verde túnica la ampara,
hasta que Ceres borda su vestido
con estrellas doradas.

Aún antes de existir, su augusta madre
el vegetal imperio le prepara,
y por regio blasón la gran diadema
la ciñe de esmeraldas.

From the fertile breast of mother earth, in an upright stance rises the proud pineapple dressed in splendor, brimming with rich pomp. Since it is born, liberal Pomona with her green tunic protects it, until Ceres trims its dress with golden stars. Even before existing, its august mother prepares the vegetable kingdom for it, and for a superb blazon the crown is ringed with emeralds.

Hyperbole is the essence of the poetic imagination, and Neruda similarly constructs a fantastic setting for his ode to an onion. He too uses a classical equation: the onion and Aphro-

dite. The linking element for this unlikely pair is not beauty
but the miracle of creation beneath the earth and beneath the
sea:

Cebolla,
luminosa redoma,
pétalo a pétalo
se formó tu hermosura,
escamas de cristal te acrecentaron
y en el secreto de la tierra oscura
se redondeó tu vientre de rocío.
Bajo la tierra
fue el milagro
y cuando apareció
tu torpe tallo verde,
y nacieron
tus hojas como espadas en el huerto,
la tierra acumuló su poderío
mostrando tu desnuda transparencia,
y como en Afrodita el mar remoto
duplicó la magnolia
levantando sus senos,
la tierra
así te hizo,
cebolla,
clara como un planeta,
y destinada
a relucir,
constelación constante,
redonda rosa de agua,
sobre
la mesa
de las pobres gentes.

Onion, luminous ball, petal by petal your beauty was formed,
scales of crystal grew on you and in the secret of the dark earth
your belly was rounded by the dew. Underground the miracle
happened and when your awkward green stem appeared, and
your leaves were born like swords in the garden, the earth ac-

cumulated its power showing your transparent nudity, and as with Aphrodite the distant sea duplicated the magnolia raising up her breasts, the earth made you, onion, clear as a planet, and destined to shine, constant constellation, round rose of water on the table of the poor.

The table of the poor has replaced the gala setting of the gods; Neruda stresses the onion's everyday function for the ordinary man, its alimentary and gastronomic value. In this context we must remember that in Chile the onion is the basic ingredient of practically every meal. Neruda's poetry retains its social function.

In a poem as highly conceptual as the "Oda a la cebolla" it is quite evident that Neruda for all his claims of simplicity, is writing within the poetic tradition. Writing for the sheer pleasure of writing, some would say, for he now seems delighted with the concept of the poem as an intellectual creation, a concept he had earlier shunned, first in favor of sincerity, then realism, and finally, social realism. Now, the word itself takes on a suggestive power for the philosophic speaker of the poems who, godlike, imaginatively creates his own reality. Back in the aesthetically oriented 1920s, under the influence of Modernism and the avant-garde, the word was emblematic: certain words had a special connotative power and were used symbolically— for example, the use of *melancolía* in the love poems: "te pareces a la palabra melancolía" (Poem XV). In *Odas elementales* the word in itself, pure and simple, is again singled out and attributed a certain importance. The "Oda al fuego" (Ode to Fire) begins with a litany of metaphors for fire; the stanza ends abruptly, and when it resumes the speaker bluntly states that he prefers the plain word itself, "fuego":

Descabellado fuego,
enérgico,
ciego y lleno de ojos,
deslenguado,
tardío, repentino

estrella de oro,
ladrón de leña,
callado bandolero,
cocedor de cebollas,
célebre pícaro de las chispitas,
perro rabioso de un millón de dientes,
óyeme,
centro de los hogares,
rosal incorruptible,
destructor de las vidas,
celeste padre del pan y del horno,
progenitor ilustre
de ruedas y herraduras,
polen de los metales,
fundador del acero,
óyeme,
fuego.

Arde tu nombre,
da gusto
decir fuego . . .

Frenzied fire, energetic, blind and filled with eyes, loose-tongued, late, sudden, star of gold, thief of wood, silent bandit, cooker of onions, famous rogue of sparks, rabid dog of a million teeth, listen to me, center of hearths, incomparable rose patch, destroyer of lives, celestial father of bread and the oven, illustrious progenitor of wheels and horseshoes, pollen of metals, founder of steel, listen to me, fire.   Your name burns, it gives pleasure to say fire . . .

This is evidently not a paean to the hermetic imagery of *Residencia en la tierra.* Rather the series of elaborate epithets is discarded in the poem precisely because it is too hermetic, too contrived. The formula is now simplicity, and the magic word is the simplest one, in this case, fire.

The urge to simplify and to shock the reader with simplicity caused Neruda to ferret out the most outlandish subjects for his elementary odes. One is even a kitchen recipe, an ode to fish stew, the "Oda al caldillo de congrio":

Ahora
recoges
ajos,
acaricia primero
ese marfil
precioso,
huele
su
fragancia iracunda,
entonces
deja el ajo picado
caer con la cebolla
y el tomate
hasta que la cebolla
tenga color de oro.
Mientras tanto
se cuecen
con el vapor
los regios
camarones marinos
y cuando ya llegaron
a su punto,
cuando cuajó el sabor
en una salsa
formada por el jugo
del océano
y por el agua clara
que desprendió la luz de la cebolla,
entonces
que entre el congrio
y se sumerja en gloria,
que en la olla
se aceite,
se contraiga y se impregne.

Now take some garlic, first caress that precious ivory, smell its
enraged fragrance, then let the chopped garlic cook with the
onion and the tomato until the onion has the color of gold.
Meanwhile cook over steam the luscious sea shrimps and when

they are just done, when the flavor is fixed in a sauce formed by the juice of the ocean and by the clear water given off by the onion's light, then the congre should go in and let it be immersed in glory, so that in the pot it will be oiled, it will contract and be impregnated with the flavor.

There are many antecedents to this sort of poetry; Vergil's *Georgica* comes to mind with its versified advice on raising grapes and making wine. But Neruda's elementary ode is not merely didactic and practical. It contains an element of humor, a delicate whimsicality totally absent from classical and neoclassical treatments of similar subject matter. This was Neruda's charm and his undoing; for with time this lightness, this frivolity seemed a bit too much for his readers. The weight of tradition is not so easily cast off. Just as at first a few admirers insisted on "restoring" the free verses of the odes to a fixed measure of heptasyllables and hendecasyllables, later others began to voice a suspicion that the odes were less poetic than they had once thought. This criticism, mild at first, became more outspoken as Neruda began to turn out volume after volume of elementary odes. Ultimately, even his fecundity was questioned.

But just as the critics began to become concerned about what seemed to be the sameness of his elementary odes, and as Neruda seemed to be exhausting his thematic repertory, something almost predictable happened: change. In 1958, after publishing *El tercer libro de las odas,* Neruda surprised everyone with a new and different book, the paradoxically private and public conversational meanderings of *Estravagario.*

With Delia del Carril

As a "fugitive" at the time of *Canto general*

With Matilde Urrutia

Neruda in Isla Negra

7. Conversational Poetry

Estravagario

> Ahora me doy cuenta que he sido
> no sólo un hombre sino varios.   *1958*
>
> Now I realize that I have been not simply one man
> but several.

As the surge of elemental odes continued unabated, Neruda, prompted perhaps by the caviling of some readers and critics, rushed into print what he called his *Estravagario*—a very different kind of book in which he flaunted once again his extraordinary talent for change. What is remarkable is that this exquisitely prepared volume, containing a miscellany of textual and graphic material, was so totally unexpected. In August 1958, with no advance publicity, not even the usual anticipatory signals of a work in progress, *Estravagario,* inaugurating a new stage in Neruda's work, appeared on the literary scene.

The fact is that, not long after the publication of *Tercer libro de las odas* (December 1957) and fully a year before the appearance of the fourth and final book of odes, *Navegaciones y regresos* in November 1959, Losada, Neruda's regular South American publisher, brought out this volume that was so radically different in form and purpose from the series of elemental odes that readers of the time were more than a bit puzzled. In relation to Neruda's previous public posture as a writer of the people, *Estravagario* seemed very individualistic, even frivolous in its self-indulgence. What is more, the frivolity was not unintentional. Neruda pointedly closed the book with "Testamento de otoño" (Autumn Will), a lengthy last will and testament designed to update that of *Canto general*. The speaker this time, however, was pixieishly candid in his self-revision, referring not to the circumstantial particularity of his latest transformation but to the phenomenon of change in general:

De tantas veces que he nacido
tengo una experiencia salobre
como criatura del mar
con celestiales atavismos
y con destinación terrestre.
Y así me muevo sin saber
a qué mundo voy a volver
o si voy a seguir viviendo.
Mientras se resuelven las cosas
aquí dejé mi testimonio,
mi navegante estravagario
para que leyéndolo mucho
nadie pudiera aprender nada,
sino el movimiento perpetuo
de un hombre claro y confundido,
de un hombre lluvioso y alegre,
enérgico y otoñabundo.

Y ahora detrás de esta hoja
me voy y no desaparezco:
daré un salto en la transparencia
como un nadador del cielo,
y luego volveré a crecer
hasta ser tan pequeño un día
que el viento me llevará
y no sabré cómo me llamo
y no seré cuando despierte:

entonces cantaré en silencio.

Of the many times that I have been born I have a salty experience like a sea-creature with celestial atavism and with a terrestrial destiny, and thus I move on without knowing to which

world I will return or if I will go on living. While things are
being resolved I left here my testament, my navigating "estrava-
gario" so that reading it a great deal no one would ever be able
to learn anything, except the perpetual movement of a lucid
and bewildered man, of a rainy and happy man, energetic and
Autumn-minded.   And now after this page I am leaving and
I will not disappear: I'll dive into space like a swimmer in the
sky, and then I'll go on growing until I am so small one day that
the wind will carry me off and I'll not know my name and I'll
no longer be when I wake up: then I will sing in silence.

How is one to interpret this about-face, Neruda's sudden
lack of solemnity regarding himself and his work? Only eight
years before, in 1950, at the end of *Canto general,* he had
piously willed his books to the poets of tomorrow, "a los que
un día/hilarán en el ronco telar interrumpido/las signif-
icaciones de mañana" (to those who one day will weave on the
harsh interrupted loom the meanings of tomorrow, XV, xxiv,
"Testamento II"). Then, speaking as the collective voice of his
people, he went on to claim for his own work an enduring
meaning for future generations:

> Y nacerá de nuevo esta palabra,
> tal vez en otro tiempo sin dolores,
> sin las impuras hebras que adhirieron
> negras vegetaciones en mi canto,
> y otra vez en la altura estará ardiendo
> mi corazón quemante y estrellado.
>   (XV, xxviii, "Aqui termino," I Finish Here)

> And this word shall be born again, perhaps in another time
> without suffering, without the impure offshoots that dark vege-
> tation adhered to my canto, and once again in the heights my
> impassioned heart will be burning and starry.

In 1958 he makes no such claim on posterity. He does not
even ask that his writings be practical or utilitarian as in the
elemental odes; he shrugs literature off as a light entertain-

ment. Neruda's stance in *Estravagario* is that of an anti-poet. His subject is himself.

The poet's personal situation had been radically altered in the middle fifties. His literary practice came to reflect this change. In 1956 he left Delia del Carril, his constant companion since they met in Spain over twenty years before; he then married Matilde Urrutia, a Chilean with whom he had been having a clandestine affair since the late forties. *Los versos del capitán* (The Captain's Verses), an anonymous book of love poems privately printed in Naples in 1952, was a secret testimony of that love. Neruda admitted to its authorship only in 1962, when readying the second edition of his complete works for Losada. By then he had already published in Chile *Cien sonetos de amor* (One Hundred Love Sonnets, 1959), a grandiloquent public testimony of his mature love for Matilde. Although *Estravagario* is not a book of love poems, it must nevertheless be placed in this context, the socioliterary context of the author's change of life, his return to Chile, and his coming to rest in Isla Negra, his last home. Significantly, the volume's second and last poems ("Pido silencio" and "Testamento de otoño"), the only ones in which the name of Matilde is actually mentioned, serve as a referential frame, indicating that she is the subject of the other sentimental poems as well ("Con ella," "Cierto cansancio," "Amor"). Furthermore, the book was composed in 1957–58, during the course of a trip Neruda and Matilde made through Europe and the Far East. A honeymoon and a trip back in time, for the itinerary was that of the poet's early years. Poems such as "Regreso a una ciudad," "La desdichada," "Itinerarios," and "Adiós a París" chronicle the trip and the many changes wrought by time:

> En tantas ciudades estuve
> que ya la memoria me falta
> y no sé ni cómo ni cuándo.
>
> Aquellos perros de Calcuta
> que ondulaban y que sonaban

todo el día como campanas,
y en Durango, qué anduve haciendo?

Para qué me casé en Batavia?

("Itinerarios," Itineraries)

I was in so many cities that my memory fails me and I now
know neither how nor when.　Those dogs of Calcutta that
ondulated and sounded off like bells all day long, and in
Durango, what was I doing?　Why did I get married in
Batavia?

Estravagario is a very personal book. For this reason some
critics suggested it be compared to *Veinte poemas de amor.*
Others, noting a certain hermeticism, were inclined to con-
sider it in the context of *Residencia en la tierra*. Actually, the
book refuses such pat categorizations, for it contains recog-
nizable snatches of almost everything: the serendipity of the
odes, the episodic development of the epic, even a good mea-
sure of politics. The problem is that the repertory, while rec-
ognizably Nerudian, is completely reworked; everything is
treated irreverently. A political poem, for example, Neruda's
last sacred theme, deals pertly with nothing less than the side-
effects of Khrushchev's revisionism:

Todos los que me daban consejos
están más locos cada día.
Por suerte no les hice caso
y se fueron a otra ciudad,
en donde viven todos juntos
intercambiándose sombreros.

Eran sujetos estimables,
políticamente profundos,
y cada falta que yo hacía
les causaba tal sufrimiento
que encanecieron, se arrugaron,
dejaron de comer castañas,
y una otoñal melancolía
por fin los dejó delirantes.

Ahora yo no sé que ser,
si olvidadizo o respetuoso,
si continuar aconsejado
o reprocharles su delirio:
no sirvo para independiente.
Me pierdo entre tanto follaje,
y no sé si salir o entrar,
si caminar o detenerme,
si comprar gatos o tomates . . .

("Partenogénesis," Parthenogenesis)

All those who used to give me advice are crazier every day. For-
tunately I never paid much attention to them and they went
away to another city, in which they all live together swapping
hats.   They were worthy subjects, politically profound, and
every mistake that I would make caused them such suffering that
they turned gray, they wrinkled up, they gave up eating chest-
nuts, and an autumnal melancholy finally left them delir-
ious.   Now I don't know what to be, whether forgetful or re-
spectful, whether to continue being advised or to reproach them
for their madness: I cannot be an independent. I get lost in so
much foliage, and I don't know if I should get out or get in, to
go on or stop here, to buy cats or tomatoes . . .

Estravagario is important not so much for its political or
personal revision of the past as for its successful adaptation of
the tone and style of what has come to be called anti-poetry.
In this work Neruda, utilizing many of the techniques and pro-
cedures of Parra's *Poemas y antipoemas* (1954), began a whole
new stage in his own poetry and contributed to the public ac-
ceptance of a radically different type of literary expression.
Even in the few fragments of *Estravagario* poems quoted thus
far a characteristic diction is very much in evidence. Essentially
it is a colloquial mode of literary discourse, more chatty and
less reasoned than that of the elemental odes. The differences
of degree and procedure reflect the author's revised attitude
toward the function of his work. In *Odas elementales* Neruda
confidently assumed the role of philosopher and the public

responsibilities of the role; in *Estravagario* he takes a philosophic look at himself as a poet and as a man, and talks frankly to his readers as though to a circle of good friends gathered for witty after-dinner conversation. The assumption is that we share not only his concerns but his droll sense of humor as well. The poet or, rather, the anti-poet thus brings poetry down from its pedestal and, through humor, desacralizes the figure of himself as author. Hence, many poems contain mocking self-parody or declarations of authorial fickleness:

> Yo soy profesor de la vida,
> vago estudiante de la muerte
> y si lo que sé no les sirve
> no he dicho nada, sino todo.
>
> ("No tan alto," Not So High)

> I am a professor of life, roaming student of death and if what I know isn't helpful I haven't said anything, but everything.

Throughout this book we have seen how Neruda at different times and under different circumstances has been many different poets. We have noted his various, sometimes strained attempts at poetic exegesis in an effort to remold himself into one who is consistent and responsible. In *Estravagario* he sidesteps all this and jauntily refuses to be held accountable for the many turns his poetry has taken:

> Me preguntaron una vez
> por qué escribía tan oscuro,
> pueden preguntarlo a la noche,
> al mineral, a las raíces.
> Yo no supe qué contestar
> hasta que luego y después
> me agredieron dos desalmados
> acusándome de sencillo:
> que responda el agua que corre . . .
>
> (Contesta a algunos bien intencionados," He Replies
> to Some of the Well-Meaning)

> They once asked me why my writing was so obscure, they can ask the night, the mineral, the roots. I didn't know what to answer until afterward and then two soulless types came up to me accusing me of simplicity: let running water answer . . .

Now it is Neruda who recognizes the obvious: that there is no need constantly to review his past, to apologize elaborately for "errors." At this point everything is accepted and acceptable, even his enemies. Thus, a poem about Pablo de Rokha, "Tráiganlo pronto" (Bring Him Quickly), can be jocular:

> Aquel enemigo que tuve
> estará vivo todavía?
> Era un barrabás vitalicio,
> siempre ferviente y fermentando.
>
> Es melancólico no oír
> sus tenebrosas amenazas,
> sus largas listas de lamentos.
>
> Debo llamarle la atención,
> que no olvide sus andanadas,
> me gustaría un nuevo libro
> con aplastantes argumentos
> que al fin terminara conmigo.
>
> Qué voy a hacer sin forajido?
> Nadie me va a tomar en cuenta . . .

> That enemy I had can he still be alive? He was an eternal devil, always seething and fermenting.   It is melancholy not to hear his dark threats, his long lists of complaints.   I must remind him that he not forget his exploits, I would like a new book with devastating arguments that would finally finish me off.   What am I going to do without an enemy? Nobody will notice me . . .

In one sense certainly Neruda was boasting for, though Pablo de Rokha had become more reticent after the fiasco of *Neruda y Yo* (1955), other detractors began to speak out more vehemently. And in 1958, the year of *Estravagario,* a collection of pugnacious essays by Ricardo Paseyro, a former secretary of Neruda, appeared in Spain (*La palabra muerta de Pablo Neruda*). This book was soon followed by another, containing arguments for and against the poet: *Mito y verdad de Pablo Neruda* (Mexico: Asociación Mexicana por la Libertad de la Cultura, 1958). The jesting rationale of "Tráiganlo pronto" notwithstanding. Neruda was being noticed. But what seemed to be drawing the most fire now, aside from his continued membership in the Communist Party, was his supposed" irresponsibility" as an artist.

By any measure *Estravagario,* as it appeared to the reader of 1958, was a most unusual book. In it the author not only refused to take himself seriously, but he also presented his work in such a way as to challenge the reading public's sense of decorum. Readers of these poems today, as they appear in the complete works or in the paperback reprints of Losada, tend to take them all very earnestly. On the other hand, the reader of the original 1958 edition was faced with an illustrated text, a book whose outlandish engravings enhanced and contradicted the literary content. True to at least one connotation of its title,* the book was an extravaganza of sorts, containing a miscellany of literary texts both serious and comic, each illustrated with graphic material culled from diverse sources: the complete works of Jules Verne; a nineteenth-century book of objects, *Libro de objetos ilustrado* (San Luis Potosí, 1883); the pen drawings of Mexico's grim José Guadalupe Posada. One page, for example, contains a Posada sketch of a festive skeleton doing a balancing act on the back of an

---

* The title, *Estravagario,* is a wholly made-up word (like the 1923 *Crepusculario*) and suggests a collection of extravagant things. However, the term occurs only once in context ("Testamento de otoño"), where it seems to refer to the book and all it contains as a kind of navigational aid, a device for recording the position, course, and distance thus far traveled in life's uncertain journey: "Aquí dejé mi testimonio, / mi navegante estravagario" (Here I left my testimonial, my navigating *estravagario*).

emaciated circus horse. Appropriately, this illustration faces "No tan alto," an anti-poem whose subject is the sobering reality of death as a balancing force in life. The Quevedian formula of *Residencia en la tierra* is thus given a macabre twist:

> De cuando en cuando y a lo lejos
> hay que darse un baño de tumba.
>
> Sin duda todo está muy bien
> y todo está muy mal, sin duda.
>
> Van y vienen los pasajeros,
> crecen los niños y las calles,
> por fin compramos la guitarra
> que lloraba sola en la tienda.
>
> Todo está bien, todo está mal . . .

> From time to time and from afar it is necessary to take a tomb-bath.   Without doubt everything is very good and everything is very bad, without doubt.   The passengers come and go, children and streets grow, finally we bought the guitar that was crying alone in the store.   Everything is good, everything is bad . . .

In the interplay of text and illustration a new kind of poetry is born. And, although Neruda adopted the rhetoric of the anti-poem from Parra, Parra ultimately came to acknowledge the appropriateness of the graphic complement in his own *Artefactos* (1971), poems printed like postcards combining text and illustration. The purpose was the same: to go beyond the linguistic frame of literature. This is not to say that the anti-poem as practiced by Parra and Neruda lacks a literary form. Quite the contrary; the illustration enhances the text by playing against it. In this way the special effects of the assemblage, created for the most part with standard literary devices, are more directly noticeable. In the above-cited fragment of "No tan alto," for example, the vacuous formulas of the opening lines take on meaning only at the end of the phrase, when an incongruent term—"tumba," tomb—is appended to an otherwise familiar admonition: "De cuando en cuando . . . hay que darse un baño de tumba" (From time to time it is necessary to take a tomb-bath). The anti-poem makes original use of such ready-made phrases and relies on the loose, even sloppy sentence structure of ordinary speech in order to achieve its most telling effects. A case in point, also in the example above, is the pairing of asymmetrical predicate nouns with the same verb ("crecen los niños y las calles," children and streets grow). The unusual is bonded to the familiar. Finally, the illusion of spoken language is a carefully contrived artifice relying on repetition and inversion for its effectiveness ("Sin duda todo está muy bien / y todo está muy mal, sin duda"—Without doubt everything is very good and everything is very bad, without doubt). The halting contradictions implied in the conversationally stylized text are, in turn, confirmed by the visual epigraph of a festive skeleton. In this way, the combination of text and illustration interrelate to create a total composition, a printed artifact of a sort. *Estravagario,* taken as a whole, is an assortment of such artifacts.

The volume's first composition, which in Neruda's work usually serves as a kind of bellwether for what is to follow, is the only untitled item. To give it a title is to announce it as art; without a title it first engages our attention as though it were not. The graphic presentation is again important for the composition's total effectiveness. On the left-hand page there is a vertical column of hands, the familiar pointer-hands of most European and South American transit systems: ☞ They are eleven in all and fill the page from top to bottom. They point to the right-hand page, largely blank, in whose upper third there is a kind of word-ladder. To make any sense out of all this the reader must pan the page from left to right, from bottom to top:

```
                                              tan
                                        si
                                  ce
                            ne
                      se
                 cielo
            al
        subir
    Para
```

Then, eyes suspended and curiosity aroused, it is only by completing the impulse to turn the page that the reader is finally able to finish the sentence:

> dos alas,
> un violín,
> y cuantas cosas
> sin numerar, sin que se hayan nombrado,
> certificados de ojo largo y lento,
> inscripción en las uñas del almendro,
> títulos de la hierba en la mañana.

> In order to get to heaven you need two wings, a violin, and so many things unnumbered, that haven't been named, certificates of a long slow eye, registration on the thorns of an almond tree, titles from the morning grass.

The poem's distribution over several pages is not a decorative caprice; it is a visual device to make the act of reading more dynamic. The perception of the composition thus becomes a voluntary act of participation in the total sign system of verbal and graphic material. In the above item, for example, some of the things one purportedly needs for a successful trip to heaven (a start in the right direction, wings, and a violin) belong to a storybook reality; others are complex word-puzzles with a vaguely official ring: certificates, registry, titles. Documentation of course, but of what? Here the loose syntax of colloquial speech is used at the conclusion of the sentence in order to join the absurd to the logical. In the process a series of anti-images emerge, whose total meaning can only be imaginatively grasped in the overall context of the composition, playfully ridiculing heaven's impossible entrance requirements. Reading is a participatory act; and the poem is a kind of intellectual puzzle. The column of hands even suggests that it is a game.

One of the fundamental breakthrough concepts of Parra's anti-poetry that Neruda has made his own in *Estravagario* is the recognition that poetry, like other literary genres, need not be so solemn; it can be an entertainment. Whether printed in newspaper columns or in luxurious volumes, poetry is read primarily for aesthetic pleasure. Recognizing this literary fact of life, the author does not preach in *Estravagario*. He asks only that we allow him to work on our minds, to entertain us for a while. Thus, to read any poem in *Estravagario* requires the same "suspension of disbelief" as for a spectator at the performing arts. In a sense, each composition is a performance, requiring a flight of the imagination on the part of the reader. For each poem the point of departure for this flight into fancy is the illustration which precedes the text and serves as a kind of visual epigraph. The reader-viewer is thus guided into the total imaginative construct the author has provided. The extraordinary in this way does not take on the air of the ordinary; it is kept extraordinary. In this context it is well to recall the closing verses of *Estravagario,* where the speaker made the wild announcement that after the book's last page he was diving off into clear space: "Y ahora detrás de esta hoja . . . daré un salto en la transparencia."

One thing above all else is evident in this book: from beginning to end it is playful. The author is performing, holding forth as though at a party, and we reader-spectators are asked to join in the fun, provided of course that we do not interrupt. The entertainer after all knows what he is up to. Thus, in order to maintain a certain dramatic tension, some compositions are addressed to us in the plural as negative interjections ("No me pregunten," Don't Ask Me; "No me hagan caso," Don't Mind Me), while yet others call directly for our continued attention ("A callarse," Let's Be Quiet; "Pido silencio," "I Ask for Silence). In "Pido silencio," the volume's first titled poem, the speaker-performer's monologue is about to begin and we are forewarned that henceforth we may have to get along without the benign old philosopher-poet to whom we have become accustomed:

> Ahora me dejen tranquilo.
> Ahora se acostumbren sin mí.

> Now leave me alone. Now get accustomed to being without me.

A French horn is the appropriate visual epigraph for this verbal blast. For "A callarse" it is a padlock; the text begins with the familiar "let's count" formula of self-control:

> Ahora contaremos doce
> y nos quedamos todos quietos.

> Por una vez sobre la tierra
> no hablemos en ningún idioma,
> por un segundo detengámonos,
> no movamos tanto los brazos.

> Sería un minuto fragante,
> sin prisa, sin locomotoras,
> todos estaríamos juntos
> en una inquietud instantánea ...

> Now let's count to twelve and we'll all be still.   For just once on earth let's not speak in any language, for one second let's stop, let's not move our arms so much.   It would be a notorious minute, without any hurry, without locomotives, we would all be together in an instantaneous concern ...

In this piece, surprisingly enough, the speaker proposes not social solidarity but individual liberation—hence, the subtlety

of the padlock motif.* The poet's personal claim on liberty
is given added emphasis at the end through a striking varia-
tion of his opening formula:

> Ahora contaré hasta doce
> y tú te callas y me voy.

> Now I'll count to twelve and you be quiet and I'll move on.

Throughout *Estravagario* Neruda is striving for special
effects. Just as the visual epigraph in each composition is care-
fully chosen to arouse the reader's imagination at the outset so
also is each text made to conclude in a forceful way. In poem af-
ter poem the conversational rambling and colloquial informal-
ity suddenly comes to a halt; a one- or two-line variation is in-
troduced and the closing is strikingly, often rhetorically, terse.
Echo effects are sometimes created, leaving a strong and linger-
ing impression on the reader. In the above verses, for example,
the imbalance of the closing statement, lacking the subject pro-
noun ("yo," I), adds force to the finale as one mentally sup-
plies what is missing: "tú te callas y (yo) me voy."

In some of the no-nonsense compositions the closure has a
loftily resonant quality, while in the jesting poems it can be
abruptly discordant. These are all calculated effects. An ex-
ample of a particularly resonant finale is found in a moving
memory-poem, "La desdichada" (The Unlucky One), evoking
Josie Bliss, whom Neruda abandoned in Burma during the
Residencia epoch. An aura of finality is imparted to the buried
past, as strophe after strophe layers on details marking the re-
lentless passage of time. Then, exactly midway through the
poem, an odd verse of a single line in the imperfect tense eerily
links the absolute past to the present of narration. It is as

---

*In 1957, while in Paris with Matilde, Neruda was interviewed in *France
Observateur* (October 24, 1957). As though laying the groundwork for a
new stage in his writing, he categorically declared: "I don't believe that
poetry should be exclusively social."

though everything passed away with time, but the woman, or rather the memory of her, refused to die: "Y aquella mujer no moría" (And that woman didn't die). This image, powerful at the poem's midpoint, takes on an additional force at the end where it reappears in a slightly modified form: "Y aquella mujer esperando" (And that woman waiting). In order to appreciate the special contextual significance of these particular lines it is only necessary to read the poem through:

> La dejé en la puerta esperando
> y me fui para no volver.
>
> No supo que no volvería.
>
> Pasó un perro, pasó una monja,
> pasó una semana y un año.
>
> Las lluvias borraron mis pasos
> y creció el pasto en la calle,
> y uno tras otro como piedras,
> como lentas piedras, los años
> cayeron sobre su cabeza.
>
> Entonces la guerra llegó,
> llegó como un volcán sangriento.
> Murieron los niños, las casas.
>
> Y aquella mujer no moría.
>
> Se incendió toda la pradera.
> Los dulces dioses amarillos
> que hace mil años meditaban
> salieron del templo en pedazos.
> No pudieron seguir soñando.
>
> Las casas frescas y el verandah
> en que dormí sobre una hamaca,
> las plantas rosadas, las hojas
> con formas de manos gigantes,
> las chimeneas, las marimbas,
> todo fue molido y quemado.
>
> En donde estuvo la cuidad
> quedaron cosas cenicientas,

hierros torcidos, infernales
cabelleras de estatuas muertas
y una negra mancha de sangre.

Y aquella mujer esperando.

I left her in the doorway waiting and I went away for
good.   She didn't know I would not return.   A dog passed,
a nun passed, a week and a year passed.   The rains washed
away my tracks and grass grew in the street, and one after an-
other like stones, like slow stones, the years fell down upon her
head.   Then the war came, it arrived like a volcano of
blood. Children and houses died.   And that woman didn't
die.   The grass burned up. The sweet yellow gods who had
been meditating for a thousand years went out of the temple in
pieces. They couldn't go on dreaming.   The airy houses and
the verandah where I slept in a hammock, the rosy plants, the
leaves with the shapes of huge hands, the hearths, the marimbas,
everything was crushed and burned.   And where the city had
been only ashes remained, and twisted iron, infernal hairpieces
of dead statues and a black bloodstain.   And that woman
waiting.

Here, a dangling participle—"esperando"—wields a haunt-
ingly evocative power.

Throughout *Estravagario* colloquial infractions of gram-
mar common to ordinary speech are employed as sophisticated
rhetorical devices to gain the reader's attention. A blatantly
incorrect form, "sintigo" (without you, a metaplasmic per-
severance of "contigo," with you), is creatively summoned for
a special effect at the conclusion of "CantaSantiago" (Sing-
Santiago). The poem is a lengthy encomium to Chile's cap-
ital; the poet, having returned from his wanderings, grandil-
oquently evokes the city, its ugliness as well as its beauty. The
imagery is organized around the idea that the speaker needs
this city; it is a part of him and he of it. The poem winds down
in this forcefully rhetorical way:

Si, Santiago, soy una esquina
de tu amor siempre movedizo

como entusiasmos de bandera
y en el fondo te quiero tanto
que sufro si no me golpeas,
que si no me matas me muero
y no sólo cuento contigo
sino que no cuento sintigo.

Yes, Santiago, I am a streetcorner of your ever-changing love like the fluttering of a flag and down deep I love you so that I suffer if you don't hit me, and if you don't kill me I die and not only do I count on you but I don't count without you.

The graphic accompaniment to "CantaSantiago" is fitting: a quaint engraving of top-hatted citizens ceremoniously shaking hands on a streetcorner. For "La desdichada" it is staid: a woman alone, knitting. On the other hand, for a frivolous poem like "Bestiario" (Bestiary), a pastiche of amateurish animal drawings precedes a text in which Neruda pompously holds forth on what one can learn from conviviality with fleas, frogs, and pigs (among other living things). At the poem's conclusion, he takes his leave; he is off to speak with a horse, or is it a cat?

Por eso, señores, me voy
a conversar con un caballo,
que me excuse la poetisa
y que el profesor me perdone,
tengo la semana ocupada,
tengo que oír a borbotones.

Cómo se llamaba aquel gato?

Therefore, gentlemen, I am going to converse with a horse, may the poetess excuse me and may the professor pardon me, I'll be busy all week, I have to listen torrentially.   What was the name of that cat?

Again, a standard locution is altered for a special effect: a cliché of ordinary speech, "hablar a borbotones" (to speak torrentially) becomes "oír a borbotones." The misapplication of the verb, like everything else in this poem, has a humorous effect. In this way too a ludicrous atmosphere can be generated even at the outset of a piece, as in "Por boca cerrada entran las moscas" (Through a Closed Mouth Flies Enter). The title is a calculated malapropism. And, lest the reader fail to notice, sandwiched between colloquial title and text is an outrageous sketch of a young man whose mouth is tightly gagged. The text consists primarily of a rapid-fire sequence of twenty-three childlike questions on the order of why are leaves green, why does smoke rise, and so on, followed by a sublimely discursive last strophe. Only the closure is mordant:

> . . . dónde van a morir los pájaros?
> Y por qué son verdes las hojas?
>
> Es tan poco lo que sabemos
> y tanto lo que presumimos
> y tan lentamente aprendemos,
> que preguntamos, y morimos.
> Mejor guardemos orgullo
> para la ciudad de los muertos
> en el día de los difuntos
> y allí cuando el viento recorra
> los huecos de tu calavera
> te revelará tanto enigma,
> susurrándote la verdad
> donde estuvieron tus orejas.

. . . where are the birds going to die? And why are leaves green? What we know is so little and so much what we assume and so slowly do we learn, that we question, then we die. It would be better were we to conserve our pride for the city of the dead on the day of the dead and then when the wind blows through the holes in your skull it will reveal such enigmas to you, whispering the truth to you where your ears once were.

The departure from the colloquial mode and the mid-strophe shift of person, from "we" to "you," turn this otherwise light poem around, making it appear grave. Or so it would seem. However, the visual epigraph is there to remind us that it is all in jest. Indeed, the pithy finale is a kind of black humor; the punch line makes the point that nothing, save death, is to be taken seriously.

Neruda does not even take himself seriously. In a reflective poem like "Sobre mi mala educación" (On My Bad Manners) he goes out of his way to chonicle his social blunders. And with a subject as serious and as timely as his separation from Delia del Carril he is casual and relaxed. The title, "Por fin se fueron" (They Finally Left), sets the tone, as does the illustration, an overloaded stagecoach departing with standing-room only:

> Todos golpeaban a la puerta
> y se llevaban algo mío,
> eran gente desconocida
> que yo conocía muchísimo,
> eran amigos enemigos
> que esperaban desconocerme.
>
> Qué podía hacer sin herirlos?
>
> Abrí cajones, llené platos,
> destapé versos y botellas:
> ellos masticaban con furia
> en un comedor descubierto.
>
> Registraban con gran cuidado
> los rincones buscando cosas,
> yo los encontré durmiendo
> varios meses entre mis libros,
> mandaban a la cocinera,
> caminaban en mis asuntos.
>
> Pero cuando me atormentaron
> las brasas de un amor misterioso,
> cuando por amor y piedad
> padecí dormido y despierto,
> la caravana se rompió,
> se mudaron con sus camellos.

Se juntaron a maldecirme.
Estos pintorescamente puros
se solazaron, reunidos,
buscando medios con afán
para matarme de algún modo:
el puñal propuso una dama,
el cañon prefirió un valiente,
pero con nocturno entusiasmo
se decidieron por la lengua.

Con intensidad trabajaron,
con ojos, con boca y con manos.
Quién era yo, quién era ella?
Con qué derecho y cuándo y cómo?
Con castos ojos revelaban
interioridades supuestas
y decidían protegerme
contra una incesante vampira.
Adelgazaron gravemente.
Exiliados de mi conciencia
se alimentaban con suspiros.

Pasó el tiempo y no estuve solo.

Como siempre en estas historias
mata el amor al enemigo.

Ahora no sé quiénes son:
desapareciendo un minuto
se borran de mis recuerdos:
son como incómodos zapatos
que al fin me dejaron tranquilo.

Yo estoy con la miel del amor
en la dulzura vespertina.
Se los llevó la sombra a ellos,
malos amigos enemigos,
conocidos desconocidos
que no volverán a mi casa.

They all knocked at my door and carried something of mine
away, they were unknown people that I knew very well, they

were enemy-friends who hoped to not know me.   What could
I do without hurting them?   I opened drawers, I filled plates,
I uncorked verses and bottles: they chewed away furiously in a
discovered dining room.   With great care they examined the
corners looking for things, and I found them sleeping several
months among my books, they order the cook around, they
walked all over my affairs.   But when I was tormented by the
live coals of a mysterious love, when for love and pity I suffered
awake and asleep, the caravan was broken up, they moved off
with their camels.   They got together to curse me. Those
typical purists amused themselves, in company, zealously looking
for the means to kill me in some way: one woman proposed a
dagger, a bully preferred a gun, but with nocturnal enthusiasm
they decided on their tongues.   They worked with intensity,
with eyes, mouths and hands. Who was I, who was she? With
what right and when and how? With chaste eyes they would re-
veal supposed intimacies and they decided to protect me against
a relentless vampire. Gravely they wasted away. Exiled from
my mind they fed on sighs.   Time passed and I was not
alone.   As always in these stories love kills off the en-
emy.   Now I don't know who they are: disappearing in a
moment they are erased from my memory: they are like uncom-
fortable shoes that in the end no longer bothered me.   I am
now with the honey of love in the sweetness of the early evening.
The darkness carried them off, awful enemy friends, well-known
strangers who shall never get back into my house.

Only briefly, in the last strophe, referring to the bliss of his
present situation, does the poet-performer permit himself a
nonposturing aside ("Yo estoy con la miel de amor / en la
dulzura vespertina"). It almost seems like a slip of the tongue,
since the rest of the poem, for all its feigned casualness, is so
elaborately structured around the behavior of others. Those
who come to the poet's door do not carry gifts; they carry
things off. All his acquaintances are unknown; he has known
them for a long time. Even his friends are enemies. This is
the world in reverse. But Neruda refuses to take it seriously—
at least in the poem. His attitude is that of an anti-poet; he
prefers to ironize or ridicule what is personal.

Occasionally he is fanciful, as in "Fábula de la sirena y los borrachos" (Fable of the Mermaid and the Drunkards), an unpunctuated single-strophe poem with a nonstop narrative delivery:

Todos estos señores estaban dentro
cuando ella entró completamente desnuda
ellos habían bebido y comenzaron a escupirla
ella no entendía nada recién salía del río
era una sirena que se había extraviado
los insultos corrían sobre su carne lisa
la inmundicia cubrió sus pechos de oro
ella no sabía llorar por eso no lloraba
no sabía vestirse por eso no se vestía
la tatuaron con cigarrillos y con corchos quemados
y reían hasta caer al suelo de la taberna
ella no hablaba porque no sabía hablar
sus ojos eran color de amor distante
sus brazos construídos de topacios gemelos
sus labios se cortaron en la luz del coral
y de pronto salió por esa puerta
apenas entró al río quedó limpia
relució como una piedra blanca en la lluvia
y sin mirar atrás nadó de nuevo
nadó hacia nunca más hacia morir.

All these men were inside / when she entered completely nude / they had been drinking and they began to spit at her / she didn't understand anything she had recently come out of the stream/ she was a mermaid who had lost her way / the insults ran over her smooth flesh / filthiness covered her breasts of gold / she didn't know how to cry therefore did not cry / she didn't know how to dress herself therefore she did not get dressed / they tattooed her with cigarettes and with burned corks / and they laughed until they fell on the barroom floor / she did not speak because she didn't know how to talk / her eyes were the color of distant love / her arms constructed of matching topazes / her lips were cut from the light of coral / and suddenly she left by that door / scarcely had she entered the stream than she was cleansed / she shone like a white stone in the rain / and without looking back she began to swim again / she swam toward nothing more toward dying.

Whether or not Matilde is the subject (as some maintain), the parameters of the poem are not in the purview of reality and personal experience, but of the imagination. Neruda has abandoned literary realism. Having done so, he can even place himself, Cortázar-like, in the realm of the fantastic:

> Casi pensé durmiendo,
> casi soñé en el polvo,
> en la lluvia del sueño.
> Sentí los dientes viejos
> al dormirme, tal vez
> poco a poco me voy
> transformando en caballo...

I almost thought while sleeping. I almost dreamt in the dust, in the rain of sleep. I felt my old teeth as I dozed off, perhaps little by little I am changing into a horse ...

It is easy to see why *Estravagario* was such an odd book for its readers in 1958. In the context of Neruda's oeuvre at the time it occupied a class by itself. Only with the passage of time has it become possible to perceive in this volume presages of the various directions his poetry was to take in the years to follow: the chattily discursive memory-poem, for example, would culminate in *Memorial de Isla Negra* (Notes from Isla Negra, 1964), a five-volume autobiography in verse; while the more capricious art of, say, "Bestiario" would be continued in *Arte de pájaros* (The Art of Birds, 1966); and the stagey quality of certain fantasy poems ("Fábula de la sirena y los borrachos," "Furiosa lucha de marinos con pulpo de colosales dimensiones") would later be developed into a full-fledged verse drama, *Fulgor y muerte de Joaquín Murieta* (Splendor and Death of Joaquín Murieta, 1967). A poetry directly concerned with the here and now would also appear from time to time, coinciding with international crises: the Cuban Revolution in *Canción de gesta* (Chanson de geste, 1960); Vietnam and the generally deplorable state of the world in *Fin de mundo* (World's End, 1969); Nixon in *Incitación al Nixonicidio y alabanza de la la Revolución Chilena* (Incitement to Nixon-icide and Praise of the Chilean Revolution, 1973).

The fact is that after *Estravagario* Neruda began to write and publish at a phenomenal pace: nineteen books of poetry in just fifteen years, plus nine more posthumously. All this work remains to be studied; time and space prevent my doing so in this brief treatment of his major works. For this later production another volume and another critical approach would be required.

Estravagario marks a high point in Neruda's life and art. With this book he freed his writing from his own literary tra-dition, at the same time that he managed to free his person from his social, political, and literary past. Equipped with the col-loquial diction of the anti-poem and the liberated attitude of the anti-poet, he was able to strike out in many diverse direc-tions. Neruda recognized the epochal nature of this, the final stage of his development as a man and as a writer; in one of the more histrionic poems of *Estravagario,* "El miedo" (Fear), he even referred to himself by name. Dismissing all those who would intrude in his life or work, he announces that henceforth he will answer only to himself:

> Por eso en estos cortos días
> no voy a tomarlos en cuenta,
> voy a abrirme y voy a encerrarme
> con mi más pérfido enemigo,
> Pablo Neruda.

Therefore in these short days I am not going to pay any atten-tion to them, I am going to open myself up and close myself in with my most perfidious enemy, Pablo Neruda.

And so he did.

Selected Bibliography

Listed here are the books and articles which I have found to be most useful in the preparation of this guide to Neruda's major works. For a more complete listing of Nerudiana, the reader will need to consult several overlapping bibliographies: *Pablo Neruda: Bibliografía selectiva* (Santiago, Biblioteca del Congreso, 1971); Hernán Loyola, "La obra de Pablo Neruda: Guía bibliográfica," and Alfonso Escudero, "Fuentes para el conocimiento de Pablo Neruda" (both in Volume III of *Obras completas* [Buenos Aires, Losada, 1973]); Horacio Jorge Becco, *Pablo Neruda: Bibliografía* (Buenos Aires, Casa Pardo, 1975). Also, in 1974, following Neruda's death much valuable material not yet registered in any bibliography appeared in several homages, notably those of *Cuadernos Hispanoamericanos*, *Insula, Europe, Modern Poetry Studies,* and *Review '74*.

A. Books on Neruda

Aguirre, Margarita. *Las vidas de Pablo Neruda*. Santiago, Zig-Zag, 1967.

Alazraki, Jaime. *Poética y poesía de Pablo Neruda*. New York, Las Américas, 1965.

Aldunate Phillips, Arturo. *El nuevo arte poético y Pablo Neruda*. Santiago, Nascimento, 1936.

Alone (Hernán Díaz Arrieta). *Los cuatro grandes de la literatura chilena*. Santiago, Zig-Zag, 1962.

Alonso, Amado. *Poesía y estilo de Pablo Neruda*. Buenos Aires, Losada, 1940.

Augier, Angel, and others. *Homenaje cubano a Pablo Neruda*. Havana, Palacio Municipal, 1948.

Bellini, Giuseppe. *La Poesia di Pablo Neruda*. Padua, Garangola, 1966.

Cardona Peña, Alfredo. *Pablo Neruda y otros ensayos*. Mexico, Andrea, 1955.

Concha, Jaime. *Neruda 1904–1936*. Santiago, Universitaria, 1972.

Fernández Larraín, Sergio. *Cartas de amor de Pablo Neruda*. Madrid, Rodas, 1974.

García Lorca, Federico, and others. *Homenaje a Pablo Neruda*. Madrid, Plutarco, 1935.

Loveluck, Juan, and others. *Simposio Pablo Neruda: Actas*. New York, Las Américas, 1975.

Loyola, Hernán. *Ser y morir en Pablo Neruda*. Santiago, Editora Santiago, 1967.

Lozada, Alfredo. *El monismo agónico de Pablo Neruda*. Mexico, Costa-Amic, 1971.

Marcenac, Jean. *Pablo Neruda*. Paris, Seghers, 1954.

Melis, Antonio. *Neruda*. Florence, Castoro, 1970.

Montes, Hugo. *Para Leer a Neruda*. Buenos Aires, Francisco de Aguirre, 1974.

Neruda, Pablo. *Confieso que he vivido*. Buenos Aires, Losada, 1974.

Riess, F. T. *The Word and the Stone*. London, Oxford, 1972.

Rivero, Eliana. *El gran amor de Pablo Neruda*. Madrid, Plaza Mayor, 1971.

Rodman, Selden. *South America of the Poets*. New York, New Directions, 1970.

Rodríguez Monegal, Emir. *El viajero inmóvil*. Buenos Aires, Losada, 1966.

Rokha, Pablo de. *Neruda y yo*. Santiago, Multitud, 1955.

Salama, Roberto. *Para una crítica de Pablo Neruda*. Buenos Aires, Cartago, 1957.

Sicard, Alain. *La Pensée Poétique de Pablo Neruda*. Lille, Université de Lille, 1977.

Siefer, Elisabeth. *Epische Stilelemente im* Canto general. Munich, Wilhelm Fink, 1970.

Silva Castro, Raúl. *Pablo Neruda*. Santiago, Universitaria, 1964.

Tijonov, Nicolai, and others. *Pablo Neruda: Poeta y combatiente*. Moscow, Soviet Academy of Sciences, 1974.

Yurkievich, Saúl. *Fundadores de la nueva poesía hispanoamericana*. Barcelona, Barral, 1971.

B. *Articles on Neruda*

Alberti, Rafael. "De mon amitié avec Pablo Neruda," *Europe*, 419–420:71–75 (March–April 1964).

Alegría, Fernando. "Two Worlds in Conflict," *Berkeley Review*, 1:27–41 (1957).

Alone (Hernán Díaz Arrieta). *"Estravagario,* por Pablo Neruda," *El Mercurio* (Santiago), December 21, 1958.

——— "Muerte y transfiguración de Pablo Neruda," *El Mercurio* (Santiago), January 30, 1955.

——— "Pablo de Rokha y Pablo Neruda," *El Mercurio* (Santiago), March 28, 1964.

——— *"Tentativa del hombre infinito,* por Pablo Neruda," *La Nación* (Santiago), January 10, 1926.

——— *"Veinte poemas de amor y una canción desesperada,"* *La Nación* (Santiago), August 3, 1924.

Asturias, Miguel Angel. "Un mano a mano de Nobel a Nobel," *Revista Iberoamericana* 82–83:15–20 (January–June 1973).

Belitt, Ben. "The Burning Sarcophagus: A Revaluation of Pablo Neruda," *Southern Review,* Summer (July 1968).

Benedetti, Mario. "Vallejo y Neruda: dos modos de influir," *Casa de las Américas,* 7:91–93 (July–August 1967).

Bly, Roger. "Pablo Neruda: An Interview," *Book Week* (New York) August 14, 1966.

Cantón, Wilberto. "Pablo Neruda en México (1940–1943)," *Anales de la Universidad de Chile,* 157–160:263–269 (January–December 1971).

Cardona Peña, Alfredo, "Pablo Neruda: Breve historia de sus libros," *Cuadernos Americanos,* 6:257–289 (December 1950).

Concha, Jaime. "Interpretación de *Residencia en la tierra,"* *Mapocho,* 2:5–39 (July 1963).

——— "Los orígenes (la primera infancia de Neruda)," *Revista Iberoamericana,* 72:389–406 (July–September 1970).

——— "Sexo y pobreza," *Revista Iberoamericana,* 82–83:135–157 (January–June 1973).

Cortázar, Julio. "Carta abierta a Pablo Neruda," *Revista Iberoamericana,* 82–83:21–26 (January–June 1973).

Cortínez, Carlos. "Fidelidad de Neruda a su visión residenciaria," in *Fantasía y realismo mágico en Iberoamérica* (Lansing, Michigan State University, 1975), pp. 177–183.

Chocano, José Santos. "Panorama lírico (a través de un recital poético)," *La Prensa* (Buenos Aires), March 12, 1933.

Délano, Luis Enrique. "Regreso de Neruda," *El Mercurio* (Santiago), May 15, 1932.

Díaz, Ramón. "Pasos entre las dos *Residencias* de Neruda," *Papeles de Son Armadans,* 54:229–242 (1969).

Selected Bibliography

Dussuel, Francisco. "*Odas elementales* de Pablo Neruda," *El Diario Ilustrado* (Santiago), February 27, 1955.

Ehrenburg, Ilya. "La poesía de Pablo Neruda," in Neruda, *Poesía política* (Santiago, Austral, 1953), pp. 11–14.

Ellis, Keith. "Poem XX, A Structural Approach," *Romance Notes*, 11:507–517 (1970).

Eshleman, Clayton. "Neruda: An Elemental Response," *Tri-Quarterly*, 15:228–237 (1969).

Felstiner, John "La danza inmóvil, el vendaval sostenido: *Four Quartets* de T. S. Eliot y *Alturas de Macchu Picchu*," *Anales de la Universidad de Chile*, 157–160:177–195 (January–December 1971).

———— "Neruda in Translation," *Yale Review* (Winter 1972), pp. 226–251.

Figueroa, Esperanza. "Neruda en inglés," *Revista Iberoamericana*, 82–83:301–347 (January–June 1973).

Finlayson, Clarence. "Paisaje en Neruda," *Atenea*, 160:47–60 (October 1938).

Foxley, Carmen. "Estructura progresivo-reiterativo en *Odas elementales*," *Taller de Letras*, 2:25–39 (1972).

Fuenzalida, Héctor. "*Odas elementales*," *Anales de la Universidad de Chile*, 100:172–175 (1955).

García-Abrines, Luis. "La forma de la última poesía de Neruda," *Revista Hispánica Moderna*, 25:303–311 (October 1959).

Giordano, Jaime. "Introducción al *Canto general*," *Mapocho*, 2:210–216 (1964).

Gómez de la Serna, Ramón. "Neruda, grandísimo poeta," *Saber Vivir* (Buenos Aires), 37 (August 1943).

González Vera, José Santos. "Disquisiciones sobre Neruda," *El Mercurio* (Santiago), November 23, 1924.

Gullón, Ricardo. "Relaciones Pablo Neruda–Juan Ramón Jiménez" *Hispanic Review*, 39:141–166 (April 1971).

Halperin, Maurice. "Pablo Neruda in Mexico," *Books Abroad*, 15: 164–168 (Spring 1941).

Jaimes Freyre, Mireya. "Neruda, poeta revolucionario," in *Fantasía y realismo mágico en Iberoamérica* (Lansing, Michigan State University, 1975), pp. 204–207.

Lago, Tomás. "Neruda en la época de *Crepusculario*," *Pro-Arte* (Santiago), December 9, 1948.

Latcham, Ricardo. "Diagnóstico de la nueva poesía chilena," *Sur*, 3:138–154 (Winter 1931).

Loveluck, Juan. "*Alturas de Macchu Picchu,* Cantos I-V," *Revista Iberoamericana,* 82–83:175–188 (January–June 1973).

——— "*Crepusculario* en su medio siglo," in *Fantasía y realismo mágico en Iberoamerica* (Lansing, Michigan State University, 1975), pp. 167–175.

Loyola, Hernán. "Los modos de autorreferencia en la obra de Pablo Neruda," *Aurora* 1:64–125 (July–December 1964).

Lozada, Alfredo. "*Residencia en la tierra,* algunas correcciones," *Revista Hispánica Moderna,* 30:108–118 (1964).

Luigi, Juan de. "Odas elementales, Nuevas odas elementales, y Odas al pícaro ofendido," *Ultima hora* (Santiago), February 3, 1957.

Marín, Juan. "Madrid-Temuco, ida y vuelta," *Ercilla* (Santiago), February 11, 1938.

Meléndez, Concha. "Pablo Neruda en su extremo imperio," *Revista Hispánica Moderna,* 3:1–32 (October 1936).

——— "Pablo Neruda, *Tercera residencia,*" *Asomante,* 6:94–96 (April–June 1950).

Meo Zilio, Giovanni. "Influencia de Sabat Ercasty en Pablo Neruda," *Revista Nacional* (Montevideo), 202:589–625 (October–November 1959).

Meza Fuentes, Roberto. "Perfil de un poeta," *El Mercurio* (Santiago), May 22, 1932.

Mistral, Gabriela. "Recado sobre Pablo Neruda," *El Mercurio* (Santiago), April 26, 1936.

Monguío, Luis. "Introducción a la poesía de Pablo Neruda," *Atenea,* 401:65–80 (July–September 1963).

Morales, Leonidas. Fundaciones y destrucciones: Pablo Neruda y Nicanor Parra," *Revista Iberoamericana,* 72:407–423 (July–September 1970).

Murena, H. A. "A propósito del *Canto general* de Pablo Neruda," *Sur,* 198:52–58 (April 1951).

Navas Ruiz, Ricardo. "Neruda y Guillén: un caso de relaciones literarias," *Revista Iberoamericana,* 60:251–262 (1965).

Neruda, Pablo. "Algunas reflexiones improvisadas sobre mis trabajos," *Mapocho* (Santiago), 2:180–182 (1964).

——— "Defensa de Vicente Huidobro" and "Una expresión dispersa" in "Crónica de Sachka," *Claridad* (Santiago), June 1924, p. 8.

———"Memorias y recuerdos de Pablo Neruda," *O Cruzeiro Internacional* (Rio de Janeiro), January–June, 1962.

———— "Sobre una poesía sin pureza," *Caballo Verde para la Poesía* (Madrid), 1:1 (October 1935).

Ogniev, Vladimir. "La lírica de Pablo Neruda," *Literatura soviética* (Moscow), 7:172–177 (1967).

Osorio, Nelson. "Apuntes para un análisis marxista de la obra de Neruda," *Apuntes* (Santiago), 2:16–23 (1972).

Panero, Leopoldo. "Canto personal, una carta perdida a Pablo Neruda," *Indice* (Madrid), July 30, 1953.

Panero, Martín. "Neruda y España," *Taller de Letras*, 2:55–86 (1972).

Parra, Nicanor. "Discurso de bienvenida . . ." in *Discursos* (Santiago, Nascimento, 1962), pp. 9–48.

Paz, Octavio. "Pablo Neruda en el corazón," *Ruta* (Mexico), 4:24–33 (1938).

———— "Respuesta a un cónsul," *Letras de México* (August 15, 1943).

Peralta, Jaime. "España en tres poetas hispanoamericanos," *Atenea*, 421–422:37–49 (July–December 1968).

Picón Salas, Mariano. "Nueva poética de Pablo Neruda," *La Hora* (Santiago) July 7, 1935.

Polt, John. "Elementos gongorinos en "El gran oceano," *Revista Hispánica Moderna* 27:23–31 (1961).

Prado, Pedro. "Pablo Neruda y su libro *Crepusculario*," *Zig-Zag* (Santiago), October 20, 1923.

Pring-Mill, Robert. "La elaboración de la cebolla," *Actas del Tercer Congreso Internacional de Hispanistas* (Mexico, 1970), pp. 739–751.

Rama, Angel. "Evasión y arraigo de Borges y Neruda," *Revista Nacional* (Montevideo), 202:514–530 (October–December 1959).

Rodríguez Fernández, Mario. "Imagen de la mujer y el amor en un momento de la poesía de Pablo Neruda," *Anales de la Universidad de Chile,* 102:128–131 (1956).

Rodríguez Monegal, Emir. "Pablo Neruda, el sistema del poeta," *Revista Iberoamericana*, 82–83:41–71 (January–June 1973).

Sánchez, Luis Alberto. "Pablo Neruda," *Cuadernos Americanos*, 2:235–247 (1962).

Sanhueza, Jorge. "Neruda, colaborador y redactor de la revista *Claridad*," *Alerce* (Santiago), 6:6–11 (Spring 1964).

Santander, Carlos. "Amor y temporalidad en *Veinte poemas de amor*," *Anales de la Universidad de Chile,* 157–160:91–105 (January–December 1971).

Santos Chocano, José. "Panorama lírico (a través de un recital poético)," *La Prensa* (Buenos Aires), March 12, 1933.

Schwartzmann, Félix. "Silencio y palabra en la poesía de Neruda," in his *Teoría de la expresión* (Santiago, Universitaria, 1967), pp. 47–49.

Sicard, Alain. "Neruda ou la Question sans Réponses," *La Quinzaine Littéraire* (Paris), November 16, 1971.

———— "La objetivación del fenómeno en la génesis de la noción de materia en *Residencia en la tierra*," *Revista Iberoamericana*, 82–83:99–110 (January–June 1973).

Silva Castro, Raúl. "Los nuevos: Pablo Neruda," *Claridad* (Santiago), January 22, 1921.

———— "La poesía de Pablo Neruda," *Claridad* (Santiago), September 1924.

————"Una hora de charla con Pablo Neruda," *El Mercurio* (Santiago), October 10, 1926.

Spitzer, Leo. "Enumerative Style and its Significance," *Modern Language Quarterly* (June 1942), pp. 171–204.

Stackelberg, Jurgen Von. "*Estravagario*, lírica de la contradicción," *Taller de letras*, 2:111–113 (1972).

Teitelboim, Volodia. "El escritor, el político," *Taller de letras*, 2:101–104 (1972).

———— "Mirando desde la colina de los cincuenta años de Neruda," *El Siglo* (Santiago), April 11, 1954.

Undurraga, Antonio de. "Neruda al senado," *Las Ultimas Noticias* (Santiago), March 10, 1945.

Valente, Ignacio. "Residencias y Antipoemas," *El Mercurio* (Santiago), February 23, 1969.

Villegas, Juan. "Héroes y antihéroes en el *Canto general*," *Anales de la Universidad de Chile*, 157–160:139–151 (January–December 1971).

Vivanco, Luis Felipe. "La desesperación en el lenguaje," *Cruz y Raya*, (Madrid), 8:149–158 (1933).

Yurkievich, Saúl. "Realidad y poesía," *Humanidades* (La Plata), 35:251–277 (1960).

C. *Neruda in English*

Much of Neruda's poetry has been translated, several times over in the case of the more difficult works. Here, for the convenience of those who wish to read more of Neruda in English, I have appended a list of the works discussed in this volume that are currently available in translation. A more complete listing, comprising translations of individual poems as well, is contained in Hernán Loyola's "La obra de Pablo Neruda, Guía bibliográfica" (items 1228–1266), included in volume III of Neruda's *Obras completas*. For a discussion of some of the problems Neruda's diverse poetic styles have posed for his many translators it is useful to consult John Felstiner's thoughtful essay on "Neruda in Translation" *(Yale Review, Winter 1972, pp. 226–251)*.

Veinte poemas de amor y una canción desesperada (1924). Translated by W. S. Merwin as *Twenty Love Poems and a Song of Despair*. New York, Penguin, 1976.

Residencia en la tierra I–II (1935) and *Tercera residencia* (1947). Translated by Donald Walsh as *Residence on Earth*. New York, New Directions, 1973.

Alturas de Macchu Picchu, a section of *Canto general* (1950). Translated by Nathaniel Tarn as *Heights of Macchu Picchu*. New York, Farrar, 1967.

Odas elementales (1954). Translated by Carlos Lozano as *Elementary Odes*. New York, Massa, 1961.

Estravagario (1958). Translated by Alastair Reid as *Extravagaria*. New York, Farrar, 1974.

Selected Poems: A Bilingual Edition. Edited by Nathaniel Tarn. Translated by Anthony Kerrigan, W. S. Merwin, Alastair Reid, and Nathaniel Tarn. New York, Delacorte Press/Seymour Lawrence, 1972.

Five Decades: Poems 1925–1970. A one-volume selection of Neruda's major works in translation, edited by Ben Bellit. New York, Grove, 1974.

Index

References are made to persons in CAPITALS, *to titles of* individual poems in *italics,* and to the first lines of otherwise untitled poems in ordinary roman type.

Index

Index